Teen Stock Market Investing 101: A Wealth-Building Guide

Easy Tools to Navigate the Stock Market, Make Strategic Money Decisions, and Set Yourself Up for a Life of Financial Freedom

Sherri Todd

© **Copyright 2024 - All rights reserved.**

The content contained within this book may not be reproduced, duplicated or transmitted without direct written permission from the author or the publisher.

Under no circumstances will any blame or legal responsibility be held against the publisher, or author, for any damages, reparation, or monetary loss due to the information contained within this book, either directly or indirectly.

Legal Notice:

This book is copyright protected. It is only for personal use. You cannot amend, distribute, sell, use, quote or paraphrase any part, or the content within this book, without the consent of the author or publisher.

Disclaimer Notice:

Please note the information contained within this document is for educational and entertainment purposes only. All effort has been executed to present accurate, up to date, reliable, complete information. No warranties of any kind are declared or implied. Readers acknowledge that the author is not engaged in the rendering of legal, financial, medical or professional advice. The content within this book has been derived from various sources. Please consult a licensed professional before attempting any techniques outlined in this book.

By reading this document, the reader agrees that under no circumstances is the author responsible for any losses, direct or indirect, that are incurred as a result of the use of the information contained within this document, including, but not limited to, errors, omissions, or inaccuracies.

Table of Contents

INTRODUCTION 1

    MY STOCK INVESTING JOURNEY: HOW I STARTED 2
    WHY I WROTE THIS TEEN STOCK MARKET INVESTING 101 BOOK 3
    WHAT YOU'LL LEARN FROM THIS BOOK 3
        Chapter 1: Introduction to Stock Market Investing 4
        Chapter 2: Opening Your First Brokerage Account 4
        Chapter 3: Strategic Stock Market Decision-Making 4
        Chapter 4: Investment Risk Awareness and Mitigation 5
        Chapter 5: Key Financial Concepts 5
        Chapter 6: Practical Exercises for Teen Investors 5
        Chapter 7: Using Technology for Investment Research 5

CHAPTER 1: INTRODUCTION TO STOCK MARKET INVESTING 7

    INTRODUCTION TO STOCK MARKET INVESTING 7
        Benefits and Problems of Teen Investors 7
        Advantages of Beginning to Invest at a Young Age 10
        Significance of Financial Education for Teens 11
    DEMYSTIFYING STOCK MARKET BASICS 13
        Key Words to Learn in Stock Investing 13
        The Notion of Stocks Ownership 15
        How the Stock Market Works 16
    THE TEEN INVESTOR'S MINDSET 17
        Investor Anxieties and Misunderstandings 18
        Have a Proactive, Confident Attitude 19
        How Important Is Having Reasonable Expectations? 20
    KEY TAKEAWAYS 21

CHAPTER 2: OPENING YOUR FIRST BROKERAGE ACCOUNT 23

    OPENING YOUR FIRST BROKERAGE ACCOUNT 23
        Step-By-Step Guide for Opening a Brokerage Account 23
        Types of Accounts and Considerations for Teens 25
        How to Select a Trustworthy Brokerage Platform 26
    UNDERSTANDING STOCK QUOTES AND MARKET DATA 27
        What Are the Major Stock Market Indicators? 27
        Examples in Practice for Interpreting Stock Quotations 28
        Internet Resources for Monitoring Market Data 30
    DIVERSIFYING INVESTMENTS BEYOND INDIVIDUAL STOCKS 31

    Other Investing Alternatives 32
    Risk and Return of Investment Vehicles 33
    Tips on Creating a Portfolio of Varied Investments 35
  KEY TAKEAWAYS 36

CHAPTER 3: STRATEGIC STOCK MARKET DECISION-MAKING 39

  STRATEGIC STOCK MARKET DECISION-MAKING 39
    Introduction to Fundamental and Technical Analysis 39
    How to Investigate and Evaluate Various Stocks 40
    Advice for Assessing Investment Prospects 41
  TIMING THE MARKET: MYTHS AND REALITIES 42
    Common Misconceptions About Market Timing Busted 43
    Problems Involved in Trying to Time the Market 45
    Importance of Having a Lengthy Investment Perspective 46
  TYPICAL INVESTING MISTAKES TO AVOID 47
    Common Mistakes Inexperienced Investors Make 47
    How to Prevent Making Hasty Decisions 49
    Insights From Past Occurrences in the Industry 51
  KEY TAKEAWAYS 52

CHAPTER 4: INVESTMENT RISK AWARENESS AND MITIGATION 53

  INVESTMENT RISK AWARENESS AND MITIGATION 53
    Categories of Investing Hazards 53
    Risk Management and Mitigation Techniques 55
    Importance of Diversification in Risk Management 57
  CREATING LONG-TERM WEALTH 58
    How Compound Interest Affects the Growth of Wealth 58
    Real-World Instances of How the Compounding Effect Works 59
    Tips on How to Use Compound Interest to Achieve Long-Term Financial Goals 60
  SETTING FINANCIAL GOALS AND MILESTONES 61
    Guidance on Setting Short-Term and Long-Term Financial Goals 61
    How to Establish Attainable Goals 62
    Money Matters: Financial Goal-Setting 64
    The Significance of Periodically Reviewing and Modifying Objectives 65
  KEY TAKEAWAYS 66

CHAPTER 5: KEY FINANCIAL CONCEPTS 69

  KEY FINANCIAL CONCEPTS 69
    How Financial Literacy Helps People Make Wise Financial Decisions 70
    Everyday Life Examples to Illustrate Financial Principles 71
  UNDERSTANDING TAXES AND INVESTMENT IMPLICATIONS 73
    Tips on Tax-Efficient Investment Techniques 74
    Why It's Crucial to Keep Up With Tax Legislation 75

ISSUES OF ETHICS IN THE STOCK MARKET 76
  Investors' Societal Responsibilities 77
  How to Match Personal Beliefs With Financial Portfolios 79
KEY TAKEAWAYS 80

CHAPTER 6: PRACTICAL EXERCISES FOR TEEN INVESTORS 83

PRACTICAL EXERCISES FOR TEEN INVESTORS 83
  Exercises Using Simulation to Make Investing Choices............................... 85
  How to Draw Lessons From Successful and Unprofitable Financial Situations
  86
CASE STUDIES OF TEEN INVESTORS 88
  Successful Investors Who Started Stock Investing in High School 89
  Lessons Learned From the Experiences of Peer Investors........................... 90
MODIFYING INVESTMENT APPROACHES WITH TIME... 92
  Importance of Routine Review and Adjustment of Stock Portfolio.............. 93
  Case Studies Showing Successful Adjustments of Tactics Under Changing
  Market Conditions 95
KEY TAKEAWAYS 96

CHAPTER 7: USING TECHNOLOGY FOR INVESTMENT RESEARCH 99

USING TECHNOLOGY FOR INVESTMENT RESEARCH 99
  Advice on How to Use Technology to Keep Up With Industry Developments
  101
  Data Analytics and Its Role in Enhancing Investment Decisions................ 102
AUTOMATION AND ROBO-ADVISORS FOR TEENS 103
  Advantages and Restrictions of Automated Investing Services................. 104
  Tips on How to Include Tech-Driven Solutions Into Your Stock Investing
  Approach 106
CYBERSECURITY AND ONLINE SAFETY 107
  Understanding the Cyber Threat Landscape 107
  Safeguard Your Financial and Personal Information Effectively................ 110
  Suggestions for Safe Internet Conduct to Safeguard Young Investors 113
STARTING SMALL AND GROWING IT TO A LARGE ACCOUNT 114
KEY TAKEAWAYS 116

CONCLUSION...119

OBJECTIVE 1: PROVIDING A SOLID INTRODUCTION.. 119
OBJECTIVE 2: EQUIPPING YOU WITH TOOLS AND SKILLS 120
OBJECTIVE 3: INSTILLING LONG-TERM WEALTH-BUILDING.. 120

REFERENCES...123

Introduction

Imagine this: You're a teenager with a knack for scrolling through social media faster than a cheetah on a sprint. But instead of eyeing the latest TikTok dance, you're tuning into the world of stocks. Sounds like grown-up stuff, right? Well, not quite. Think of the stock market as a giant virtual shopping mall, where you're picking up pieces of companies instead of buying sneakers.

Your pocket money isn't simply cash; it's the star of this adventure. Picture this: You choose to invest in the creators of your all-time favorite video game. Why? You have the inside scoop. You've mastered the game, your friends can't stop talking about it, and even your cat seems oddly captivated. It's like you've got the cheat code to know this game will be a massive hit. Your investment isn't just a shot in the dark; it's a strategic move based on what you know and love. It's your turn to play the game—but in the stock market arena this time!

Weeks pass, and boom! The game blows up in popularity. Your friends are impressed. And your cat? Well, your cat doesn't care, but that's okay. Your small investment starts to grow, and suddenly, you're not only the teenager who's good at video games but also the savvy investor in the making.

The moral of the story? With some research and a sprinkle of courage, you can dive into the world of stocks. Your next significant investment could be in the company that makes your cat's favorite toy. Remember, the stock market can be as unpredictable as your math teacher's pop quizzes, so invest wisely!

My Stock Investing Journey: How I Started

Back in my teenage years, I stumbled into the world of stock market investing, and, oh boy, it was a rollercoaster ride—minus the safety bars! It started with a simple economics class at school. The teacher mentioned investing, and my ears perked up like a dog hearing the word *walk*.

So, armed with my babysitting money and a burning curiosity, I decided to dive into the stock market. My first investment? A small tech company that, according to my extensive research (aka a 15-minute internet search), was "going places." Spoiler alert: It didn't go to the places I thought it would. Lessons learned!

I quickly realized that investing wasn't just about picking stocks randomly. It was like a puzzle, requiring strategy, patience, and a bit of luck. I started reading more, following market trends, and learning from successful investors. I even kept a journal titled *My Stock Market Adventures*—half numbers, half teenage drama.

Then came the big win: After months of learning and a few small losses, I invested in a company developing eco-friendly packaging. My inner environmentalist was cheering. And guess what? The stock soared! I felt like the queen of Wall Street (or at least the queen of my tiny bedroom turned stock market HQ).

Winning in the stock market isn't only about watching your bank account grow (though that's a fantastic part). It's also about boosting your confidence and expanding your know-how. You get to learn the art of risk assessment, hone your gut feelings, and decode the market's ups and downs. It's super empowering, primarily as a teen navigating a world run mainly by adults. You're not simply earning money; you're gaining life skills that put you in the driver's seat. So, gear up and get ready to take control—the stock market is your playground now!

Why I Wrote This Teen Stock Market Investing 101 Book

It's simple: You're never too young to learn about money. This book is like your secret guide to the adult world of finance but way more fun. I wanted to give you the tools to confidently understand and navigate the stock market. Plus, who says learning about investments has to be boring? By the end of this book, you'll be impressing your friends (and maybe even your parents) with your savvy investment talks. So, dive in, and let's make finance your new favorite subject!

What You'll Learn From This Book

Diving into stock investing is like discovering an incredible hidden level in your favorite video game, but here, the rewards are real cash, not just points. Picture this: Your hard-earned allowance or job money could grow into something bigger. Starting as a teen gives you a tremendous advantage. You'll get the hang of tracking market trends, appreciate the art of waiting patiently, and learn to make wise money moves. This journey isn't just about piling up dollars; it's about becoming a pro at handling your finances. And let's be honest: You'll wow the grown-ups with your investment lingo. Imagine the fantastic points you'll score when your savvy investment choices hit the jackpot!

This book is your trusty guide, tailored just for you, the aspiring teen investor. Get ready to dive into a world where numbers, trends, and significant financial words start to make sense. Each chapter has easy-to-understand information, practical tips, and a sprinkle of fun to keep things interesting. Here's what you'll need to turn those dollar dreams into reality!

Chapter 1: Introduction to Stock Market Investing

Picture the stock market as a vast, intricate game, but you're playing with actual cash instead of points. This chapter is your crash course on the essentials:

- understanding what the stock market is
- grasping its mechanics
- figuring out why it matters so much

You'll journey through the market's past, get comfy with necessary jargon, and shatter some common misconceptions. Consider this your unofficial, way cooler Intro to Stock Market class that the school forgot to give you!

Chapter 2: Opening Your First Brokerage Account

Are you eager to dive into the investing pool? This chapter is your road map to opening your very own brokerage account. We'll take you on a journey, from picking the perfect broker that fits your style to decoding the various types of accounts out there. Imagine it as crafting your financial adventure park.

Chapter 3: Strategic Stock Market Decision-Making

It's time to gear up your strategy skills! In this chapter, we're diving into making intelligent, well-informed decisions. You're going to become a pro at digging into stock research, cracking the code of market trends, and choosing stocks that match what you're aiming for with your investments. Think of it as your training to become a master financial sleuth!

Chapter 4: Investment Risk Awareness and Mitigation

Just like a superhero knows their weaknesses, when it comes to investing, it's all about understanding the risks involved. This chapter will show you how to spot possible dangers and give you strategies to tackle them head-on. You'll discover the art of finding that sweet spot between risk and reward so you can confidently step into the investing world. It's like learning to navigate a thrilling adventure while keeping an eye out for potential challenges!

Chapter 5: Key Financial Concepts

This chapter is your money language guide. We'll simplify important financial ideas such as diversification, dividends, and market capitalization. Think of it as picking up a fantastic new language, but this one is all about the world of money—and trust me, it's way more fascinating!

Chapter 6: Practical Exercises for Teen Investors

Let's roll up our sleeves and dive into some real action! This chapter has exciting hands-on activities and excellent simulations to help you apply your knowledge. You'll have a blast experimenting with various investment scenarios, turning learning into a fun and interactive adventure. Get ready to be the captain of your financial ship as we navigate through these practical exercises!

Chapter 7: Using Technology for Investment Research

In today's tech-savvy world, technology becomes your trusty sidekick when investing. This chapter will introduce you to many excellent tech tools and apps that make researching investments easy. You'll discover how to wield these digital gadgets to keep yourself in the know and make intelligent choices. It's like having a toolbox of gadgets to help you on your investing superhero journey!

This is only the starting line of your exciting financial adventure. Money is like a constantly changing video game with endless levels to explore. So, keep that curiosity alive, take well-thought-out risks, and stay in the game! Your investment journey is just beginning.

It's time to hop off that couch and dive into the thrilling world of stock market investing. You have the brains, energy, and opportunity to start this exciting journey. Don't let your potential dollars sit around, gather dust, or worse, get spent on another forgettable fad. It's your money, future, and chance to make a mark in the financial universe. So, let's start learning!

Chapter 1:

Introduction to Stock Market Investing

You're making a brilliant move by stepping into the stock market game. Let's jump right into the thrilling universe of stocks, understanding market indices and unraveling the mysteries of how exchanges tick. Are you ready to squash those investing jitters and supercharge your confidence? It's time to crack open the stock market's secrets and become an investing champ!

Introduction to Stock Market Investing

Teen stock investing is like unlocking a secret level in a video game, where you can reap fantastic benefits and face tricky challenges. Starting young has its perks, and understanding money matters early on is like having a superpower. Let's explore this exciting world and why being money-smart now is a big win for your future!

Benefits and Problems of Teen Investors

Investing as a teenager comes with both exciting opportunities and significant risks. It's a world where young investors can learn valuable financial skills and face potential pitfalls. With a light-hearted yet informative lens, let's dive into the benefits and problems of teen investing.

Benefits

- **Diverse Investment Options:** Teens have a plethora of investment options. Mutual funds, ETFs, stocks, and bonds are just the start. Mutual funds offer a professionally managed portfolio, while ETFs provide a low-cost alternative. Stocks offer a more hands-on approach. Bonds are outstanding for those seeking steadier returns.

- **Learning Financial Literacy Early:** Teen investors, you're jumping into the deep end of the financial market early. Picture it as a video game where your cash and real-world effects are the score. Snagging stocks like AMC Entertainment and tracking their rollercoaster value is a hands-on, heart-pumping learning experience.

- **Preparation for Future Financial Responsibilities:** Investing as a teen is akin to taking a sneak peek at adulting. It prepares you for future financial responsibilities like budgeting, saving, and investing for long-term goals. It's like training wheels for your wallet!

- **Technological Advantage:** With apps and online platforms, teen investors are at the forefront of technological advancements in investing. You're the digital natives, surfing the waves of the stock market with a smartphone in hand.

- **Specialized Accounts:** There are investment accounts tailored for teens, like the Minor Roth IRA and UTMA accounts, which provide structured pathways to save and invest, teaching the importance of long-term planning.

Problems

- **Risk of Loss:** The stock market is not all rainbows and butterflies. The risk of losing money can be a hard lesson, especially if it's your hard-earned cash from summer jobs. Remember, not all stocks shoot to the moon like GameStop!

- **Complexity and Misinformation:** Investing can seem tricky for teens, and getting misled by wrong info is a real risk. It's not just about choosing stocks. It's about grasping stuff like how the market behaves, what those economic signs mean, and the nitty-gritty of company basics.

- **Psychological Impact:** Investing can feel like riding a rollercoaster, like having your life savings right up front! Those stock prices constantly jumping around can stress you out. But as a teen investor, it's all part of the excitement. So, gear up and prepare to handle those market ups and downs like a champ!

- **Gamification and Impulsivity:** Those trading apps with flashy push notifications and gamified tricks might lure you into trading more than you should. It's like having a credit card in a candy store—super tempting but can lead to some not-so-sweet outcomes. Stay sharp and don't let those apps play you!

- **Regulatory Concerns:** Regulators are on alert as more teens dive into investing. It's tricky to balance making finance accessible and not taking advantage of newcomers. If you're a teen stepping into this world, it's super important to know the rules and stay on top of the regulations that keep everything fair and square in finance. Stay sharp and informed!

Teen investing is like an adventurous road trip into the financial world, full of opportunities to grow and learn. But just like learning to drive, you need the proper guidance, plenty of practice, and a solid understanding of the rules. So, gear up! Dive into investing with excitement and smarts, making wise and responsible choices along the way.

Advantages of Beginning to Invest at a Young Age

Let's talk about why starting to invest at a young age is a brilliant move for your future. Think of it as planting a seed early in a garden—it has more time to grow and flourish! Here are some critical advantages backed by the latest insights and a dash of examples to clarify them:

- **The Magic of Compound Interest:** Compound interest is like a superhero for your money! Here's the deal: When you invest, your money earns interest, making even more interest. Picture this: If you start investing at 25, with an incredible 7% yearly return, you'll have way more cash for retirement than starting at 35, even if you save the same amount every year. It's like a money magic trick—the earlier you begin, the faster your money multiplies. Compound interest is your ticket to becoming a millionaire and gaining financial freedom.

- **Building a Robust Financial Safety Net:** Embarking on your financial journey early isn't just about saving funds; it involves building a financial safety net. This safety cushion becomes invaluable during life's unforeseen challenges, such as sudden medical expenses or unexpected career changes, providing reassurance and a feeling of stability. Envision it as your financial superhero, standing by to come to your aid when you face unexpected situations!

- **Learning Financial Discipline Early:** Getting into investing at a young age isn't only about growing your money; it's about getting a head start in becoming a financial pro. You'll start building your saving and budgeting skills right from the get-go, setting you up for a lifetime of making smart money choices. It's like sprinting ahead in the race to financial know-how!

- **Higher Tolerance for Risk:** As a young investor, you have a secret weapon: time. This means you can dive headfirst into exciting, high-risk investments like stocks. Why? Because you've got plenty of time to recover from any bumps in the road. Imagine it as boldly riding the investment rollercoaster, always ready to conquer every twist and turn with time as your trusty sidekick.

- **Strategic Long-Term Planning:** Starting to invest early gives you the luxury of a longer timeline. This means you can think and plan more strategically, adjusting your investment approach as your life evolves. Whether it's saving for a house, education, or a dream vacation, early starting gives you more runway to reach your financial goals.

- **Maximizing Tax-Advantaged Accounts:** You won't believe it! Starting your investment journey unlocks incredible tax-friendly accounts like 401(k)s and IRAs. These are like your undercover weapons for saving on taxes. They let your investments grow without pesky taxes until you reach retirement age. It's your clever and strategic move to supercharge your investments!

Getting a head start on investing as a young person is a brilliant move. Why? It's because of the incredible power of compound interest, which makes your money grow faster. And here's the best part: The earlier you begin, the more your money multiplies.

Significance of Financial Education for Teens

Financial education is a critical skill for teens, and the latest research and statistics highlight its growing importance. Let's delve into this topic with a light-hearted yet informative tone, focusing on why it's crucial for you, as a teen, to get savvy about finances.

Financial Literacy in the United States: A Sobering Picture

Here's something to chew on: 87% of U.S. teenagers need help understanding their finances (Rose, 2023). And it's not just teens: 63% of Americans live paycheck to paycheck. The economic consequences are significant. In 2020, Americans lost a whopping $415 billion due to poor financial literacy. That's about $1,634 per person (Radic, 2023)! Picture all the cool stuff you could buy with your extra dough—like snagging the latest smartphone or even kicking off your college fund.

The Teen Perspective

You might be thinking, *I'm just a teen. Why worry about finances now?* A survey found that 93% of teens believe financial knowledge and skills are crucial to achieving their life goals (*Survey Finds 93% of Teens Believe Financial Knowledge and Skills Are Needed*, 2022). Think about it: Whether it's saving for a car, managing student loans, or budgeting for those must-have sneakers, financial literacy is critical.

The Role of Education

Sadly, financial education isn't a staple in all schools yet. A 2022 survey showed that 35 states scored a C, D, or F for high school financial literacy (Rose, 2023). But there's a silver lining: More states are incorporating personal finance into their K–12 standards. Knowledge is power.

The Impact of Financial Illiteracy

The consequences of not knowing about money can be harsh. About 22% of U.S. adults have no emergency savings, and 30% need more to cover three months of expenses (Rose, 2023). Think about it: What would you do without savings if an unexpected expense came up, like a broken phone or a car repair?

The Digital Age and Financial Education

Here's some good news: Technology is making financial education more accessible. Programs like Greenlight offer debit cards and apps that teach crucial financial skills such as earning, saving, and investing.

Start Young, Stay Ahead

Getting a head start on financial know-how is an intelligent move. Teens with savings accounts are more inclined to attend college and become stock owners. So, whether it's cash from a part-time gig, your allowance, or birthday cash, it's time to think about handling that dough smartly. Start early and watch your financial smarts grow.

Financial smarts go beyond saving coins. They're about making intelligent choices that shape your future. Whether you learn in school, from apps, or by chatting with your folks, gaining money wisdom is a path to independence and stability. So, jump into the finance world—it's never too soon to begin!

Demystifying Stock Market Basics

Ready to decode the stock market mystery? Think of it as a giant virtual shopping mall where you can buy tiny pieces of companies, called *stocks*, through places called *exchanges*. Like a financial Hogwarts, it's magical yet logical. Let's unravel the secrets of stocks, ownership, and those enigmatic market indices.

Key Words to Learn in Stock Investing

Navigating the world of stock investing may feel like a maze of unfamiliar words and numbers, but fear not! I'm your trusty guide, here to make it easy and fun. Picture each term as a handy tool in your investment tool kit, all set to assist you in shaping your financial destiny.

- **Stocks:** Think of these as tiny slices of a company. Buying a stock means you're now a small part-owner of that company. Imagine owning a piece of a giant tech company or a famous coffee chain—that's what buying their stock feels like.

- **Bull and Bear Markets:** The market has its mood swings! When it's in a *bull market*, it's all sunshine and rising stock prices. But in a *bear market*, it's like winter, and stock prices dive.

- **Diversification:** It's like not betting everything on a single horse race. Instead, you spread your money across stocks, bonds, and mutual funds. It's like creating a money salad with a mix of ingredients to keep your finances strong and safe.

- **Compound Interest:** Investing is like planting a tree and seeing it grow. You don't only earn money on your original investment; you also accumulate on the money your investment has already made. It's like getting paid for your earnings—interest on interest!

- **Capital Gains:** This is the cash you pocket when you sell something you invested in for more than you initially put in. Think of it like finding an old, excellent car, fixing it up, and then selling it for some sweet profits!

- **Asset Allocation:** Balancing your investments is like cooking a buffet meal. You pick a little of everything that matches your preferences and your hunger. It's about finding the right mix to reach your goals and how much risk you're comfortable with.

Remember that investing is a long adventure, not a quick race. It's all about making intelligent decisions and adapting as your goals and the market shift. And remember, it's a great idea to chat with a financial expert for the best moves tailored to your situation.

The Notion of Stocks Ownership

Here's a light-hearted and informative explanation of stocks, drawing on the latest research and statistics:

Picture yourself at a massive global party where everyone is swapping pieces of paper. But hold on, these aren't just any pieces of paper—they're like mini portions of actual companies! When you grab a stock, you're not just splurging cash. You're snagging a share of that company. Pretty awesome.

Now, let's dive into some fun facts. Did you know that as of late 2023, 58% of American households owned stocks? That's a big jump from just 30% in 1989 (Jacobino & Akuffo, 2023). It's like more and more people are joining this party every year!

So, here's the lowdown on stocks: When you own a stock, you're like a mini-boss of that company. If the company's crushing it, you're raking in the dough. It's like getting a slice of the cake every time Apple sells an iPhone. But remember, if the company's struggling, your stock might feel the heat, too.

You can make money with stocks in two main ways. First, when the company's value goes up, the price of your stock increases, and you can sell it to make a profit, which is called capital appreciation. It's like grabbing a classic comic book and selling it later when it becomes a rare collector's item.

You can make money from stocks through dividends. Some companies share their profits with their shareholders, and these payouts are called dividends. It's like getting an awesome thank-you card with cash as a bonus for being a stock owner!

Now, the stock market can be a rollercoaster. For example, in 2023, there was a rally toward the end of the year, with inflation cooling down and interest rates potentially getting cut (Jacobino & Akuffo, 2023). This is where the fun—and the risk—comes in. Stock prices can go up and down based on many factors, like how the company is doing, what the economy looks like, and even news events.

Remember the January effect? It's a trend where stock prices increase in the year's first month. This happens for various reasons, such as investors buying back stocks they sold in December for tax reasons. It's like a New Year's resolution for the stock market!

Investing in stocks also means keeping an eye on the companies. For example, when a company like Hewlett Packard Enterprise acquires another company, it can boost its value. And CEO performances matter, too; they're like the captains of these giant company ships, and their decisions can rock the boat (or keep it steady).

Finally, there's something cool called Dividend Kings—companies known for consistently increasing their dividends over the years. They're like the reliable old-timers at the party, always bringing the best snacks year after year.

In a nutshell, stocks let you own a slice of a company and earn cash when the company thrives. It's a thrilling journey; but remember, it's full of highs and lows.

How the Stock Market Works

Imagine the stock market as a giant, bustling marketplace, but instead of fruits and veggies, it's packed with companies and investors. Companies like Nvidia, a tech titan, go there to sell pieces of their business, called stocks, to people who want to own a part of that company. In 2023, Nvidia's stocks soared by nearly 246%, partly thanks to its involvement in hot tech like generative AI (Enomoto, 2024).

Now, think of stocks as tickets to a rollercoaster ride. Sometimes, they go up, like Nvidia's did, and other times, they plummet. It's like a financial thrill ride! Investors buy these tickets, hoping the ride goes up and they make money.

But here's the deal: The stock market can throw curveballs and be full of surprises. In 2023, everyone braced for a recession—a significant, scary economic slowdown. However, it didn't happen! The market was like, "Psych! No recession here." Instead, some sectors, like technology, surprised investors (Enomoto, 2024).

Speaking of sectors, not all parts of the market move in sync. Some, like healthcare and utilities, weren't doing well earlier in 2023 (Adam, 2023). But as the year progressed, these "less trendy" sectors started attracting more investor interest, especially with inflation calming down.

Now, you might wonder, *What about houses and cryptocurrencies?* The housing market was downer, with sales dropping due to high mortgage rates. But cryptos? They were like the cool kids at the party, suddenly becoming popular after months of being ignored.

Here's a pro tip: Successful investing isn't just picking winners. It's also about how you buy stocks. Experts suggest using a technique called dollar-cost averaging (Adam, 2023). It means consistently investing a set amount of money, whether the market is booming or dipping. This way, you lower the chances of making a not-so-great investment simultaneously.

Keep in mind that the stock market can be a rollercoaster of emotions. When stocks drop, fear can lead to selling. When they rise, everyone rushes to buy. Picture it like a game of musical chairs: You don't want to be caught with a seat when the music stops!

So, that's the stock market for you—a mix of strategy, luck, and timing. It's like playing a sophisticated video game where the scores are real dollars. Keep your eyes on the prize, stay informed, and you might be the next prominent investor to watch out for!

The Teen Investor's Mindset

Ready to tackle the stock market with a cool head and a confident smile? Let's zap those anxious vibes and misunderstandings about investing. Embracing realistic expectations is your secret weapon to becoming a savvy, chill market master. Time to ride the investment waves with style and smarts!

Investor Anxieties and Misunderstandings

Let's dive into the world of investing, which is comparable to mastering the art of surfing. Initially, you might face some challenges, like falling off your board in the ocean. However, armed with the proper knowledge and attitude, you'll soon be riding the financial waves like a seasoned pro.

First up, understanding investor anxieties and misunderstandings is crucial. It's like deciphering a secret code; once you crack it, everything makes sense. Recent National Bureau of Economic Research findings reveal some fascinating insights (Hirshleifer, 2020).

For instance, the stock market often underreacts the publicly available information. In simple terms, this means that many investors miss out on golden opportunities because they're not paying enough attention to important clues, like a company's history of innovation or the originality of their work. It's like ignoring the secret ingredients in a winning recipe!

Speaking of recipes, let's stir some stats from a 2020 Natixis Investment Managers survey. This survey, conducted among financial professionals, shows that even during the unpredictable pandemic market, these pros weren't overly worried about long-term market performance (Goodsell, 2020). Their primary concerns were more about volatility and recession. Like the pros, stay calm during market turbulence; you can, too! It's about looking at the overall picture and not getting caught up in the short-term highs and lows.

Now, let's add a dash of advice on choosing a financial advisor. ThinkAdvisor's study found that trust and reputation play a considerable role in this decision. Around 20% of consumers trusted family recommendations, and an equal number valued the advisors' and firms' reputations (Fischer, 2021). Remember, in the financial world, trust is like currency—you want to invest it wisely! Also, don't get swayed by fancy presentations or big brand names; dig deeper to understand what the advisor can offer you.

Financial advisors are more than just numbers wizards; they're like your trusty guides on a financial adventure. They're not just about investments; they help you plan for the long run and stick to your goals. It's not only about the destination (the numbers), the exciting journey, and the innovative road map to making your dreams come true. Think of them as your financial GPS!

So, keep these points in mind:

- Stay on your toes and keep an eye on available information

- Remember, ups and downs in the market are routine

- When picking advisors, go for folks you trust who can steer you toward your long-term goals.

Have a Proactive, Confident Attitude

To succeed in stock investing as a teenager, having a go-getter attitude is a must! It's about staying informed, making smart moves, and daring to take well-thought-out risks. Let's simplify it: Being confident means you're the boss of your financial journey, making it fun and intelligent!

First, remember that anyone can invest, even with spare change. Platforms like Acorns, Greenlight, and Step make it easy for teens to start investing with as little as $1 (Sabatier, 2023). These apps offer an excellent way to ease into the world of investing. They're super easy to use and have educational materials that make learning the investing basics a breeze. The best part? You can begin with a small amount of money, thanks to features like fractional shares. You don't need a fortune to get started on your investing journey!

Investing isn't as simple as downloading an app; it's like learning a fantastic game. Picture this: You, a young earner, turning a slice of your pizza money into a million bucks! The trick is to start early. On average, folks who kick off investing at 31 miss out on $2.5 million compared to those who begin sooner (*A Teenager's Guide to Investing*, n.d.). That's a lot of missed dough!

Now, let's chat about strategy. Be proactive, which means researching, getting to know the stocks you're into, and staying updated on market trends. But don't just go with the flow. Consider the things you love and the stuff that gets you super excited. Are you a gaming enthusiast? Check out companies in that field. Are you really into fashion? Dive into retail stocks. Your hobbies can be your investment compass, making it exciting and enjoyable.

Confidence isn't about taking wild risks; it's about being smart. Use the tools and info at your fingertips. Many investment apps provide research and learning to help you make savvy moves.

Lastly, don't be afraid to make mistakes. They're part of the learning process. The most successful investors weren't born experts; they learned through experience.

How Important Is Having Reasonable Expectations?

First, remember the stock market is more like a rollercoaster than a gentle carousel. J.P. Morgan's 2024 outlook suggests that with inflation cooling to around 3.5%-4% from a sizzling 8% in 2022, things are looking up, but still expect some bumps (*Outlook 2024 Key Takeaways*, 2023). It's like expecting to win every arcade game on the first try—not going to happen.

Now, let's chat about those expectations. Think of investing like planting a tree. You don't expect a seedling to shoot up into a giant oak overnight, do you? Stocks are the same. They need time to grow. And sometimes, they might produce differently than you want them to. That's just how it goes.

J.P. Morgan's strategists say diversification is your BFF here (*Outlook 2024 Key Takeaways*, 2023). Don't put all your eggs (or dollars) in one basket. Mix it up with different stocks, bonds, and other investments. It's like having a variety of dance moves at the prom—you've got to be ready for any song!

Remember, past performance is like last year's fashion—it doesn't dictate the future. Just because a stock was the star quarterback the previous season doesn't mean it'll score touchdowns this year. Stay updated, do your homework, and consult with people who eat, sleep, and breathe stocks (like financial advisors).

And hey, losses are part of the game. It's like missing a few shots in basketball. You shake it off, learn, and keep playing. The key is not to get carried away by sky-high expectations or gloomy forecasts.

Key Takeaways

- Diving into stock market investing as a teen unlocks benefits and challenges, including learning money management and facing market risks.

- Teen investors enjoy diverse options and early financial literacy but must navigate potential loss and complexity.

- Starting young maximizes compound interest, builds financial safety nets, and teaches discipline, offering a strategic long-term view.

- Financial education for teens is vital, enhancing decision-making and preparing them for future financial responsibilities.

- Stocks represent company ownership, offering potential profits through value appreciation and dividends.

- The stock market operates as a dynamic platform for buying and selling company shares, influenced by economic and sector-specific trends.

- Teens should address common investing anxieties, maintain a proactive attitude, and set reasonable expectations for long-term success.

Now that you're armed with the 411 on stocks and exchanges and rocking a calm investor mindset, what's next? Drumroll, please. It's time to open your first brokerage account! Think of it as your gateway to the big, bold world of investing. Get ready to turn theory into action!

Chapter 2:

Opening Your First Brokerage Account

Are you eager to go on an exciting journey into the investing world? The first step is like finding a treasure chest of opportunities as you open your initial brokerage account. You'll uncover the mysteries of interpreting stock quotes and market data while mastering the skill of expanding your investments beyond just individual stocks. Let's kick-start your financial adventure!

Opening Your First Brokerage Account

Unlocking your first brokerage account opens up a world of financial opportunities. Let's explore selecting the correct account and discovering a reliable platform for your teenage investor style.

Step-By-Step Guide for Opening a Brokerage Account

Opening a brokerage account may seem daunting, but fret not! It's easier than solving a Rubik's Cube. Here's a straightforward, step-by-step guide designed just for you:

1. **Choose Your Brokerage:** Think of a brokerage as your go-to ice cream parlor. You'll want one serving of all your favorite flavors (investment choices). For newcomers, options like Fidelity, Robinhood, and TD Ameritrade (Charles Schwab acquired TD Ameritrade in November 2019) are popular. Take

some time to explore and find the one that best suits you. You may prefer a user-friendly app or scour for the most budget-friendly alternative.

2. **Gather Your Tools:** Before you start, make sure you have your Social Security number, an ID (like a driver's license), and your bank account details handy. It's like packing your backpack before a hike—you need the essentials.

3. **Fill Out the Application:** Next, you'll fill out an online application, which is as easy as creating a social media profile. You'll provide your details (rest assured, it's secure!). Share your investment background and describe your financial status.

4. **Understand Your Options:** You'll encounter different account types, like individual or joint accounts. Think of it like choosing between a solo or a multiplayer video game. Pick the one that fits your plan.

5. **Set Up Your Funding:** Connect your bank account to transfer money. It's like putting fuel in your car before a road trip. You need cash in your brokerage account to start investing.

6. **Wait for Approval:** This part requires patience, much like eagerly awaiting the delivery of your favorite pizza. Typically, it takes a few days for your account to be approved.

7. **Start Your Adventure:** Once you receive approval, you can jump headfirst into stocks, bonds, or mutual funds. Begin with a modest start by investing in a company you admire or a frequently used product.

Don't rush into buying stocks like you're grabbing the last piece of cake. Do your research, be patient, and watch your money grow.

Types of Accounts and Considerations for Teens

When it comes to investing, teenagers, there are some thrilling choices ahead! Let's explore the realm of brokerage accounts—envision them as your tools for venturing into stocks, bonds, or perhaps a portion of your beloved company.

First up, we have **custodial accounts**. These are like training wheels for your investing journey. A parent or guardian opens this account for you, but here's the cool part: any money in it is yours to invest. Imagine buying shares in a company you love, like a gaming giant or a trendy fashion brand. However, remember that your parent has the final say until you turn 18 (or 21 in some places).

Next, there's the **individual account.** This is the grown-up version you can open once you hit the magical age of 18. It's all yours—you make all the decisions (and yes, you're also responsible for them!). Picture this: You've been eyeing a tech start-up and can now invest in it directly. How cool is that?

Let's dive into a specific type of account: **education accounts**. Think of them as savings jars for your college fund. Family members can pitch in; if you use the money for education costs, it grows without taxes. It's like earning extra rewards for mapping out your future.

But wait, there's more: **retirement accounts for teens**. Yes, retirement seems light-years away, but hear me out. Accounts like a Roth IRA let you invest after-tax money now, and when you're old and gray, you get to withdraw it tax-free. It's like planting a tiny seed today and watching it grow into a giant money tree by the time you retire.

Compound interest is the secret sauce that makes your money grow faster and turns you into a millionaire when you're older. By beginning to invest in a retirement account while you're young, you're creating the ultimate money-making strategy that can lead to financial freedom and tremendous wealth for your future self.

Remember to consider fees, risks, and investment choices in all these options. And hey, always keep learning—the investing world is vast and fascinating.

How to Select a Trustworthy Brokerage Platform

Choosing a reliable brokerage platform can be as thrilling as selecting the ideal concert attire, but it might also seem daunting. Here's a brief guide to help you in making a stellar decision:

First, consider your brokerage like a trusty backpack—it must be robust, reliable, and fit all your essentials. Check for a platform regulated by big names like the SEC (Securities and Exchange Commission) in the United States or the FCA (Financial Conduct Authority) in the United Kingdom. It's like making sure a reputable brand manufactured your backpack, not a random dude selling it from the trunk of his car.

Next, look for low fees. Imagine buying a concert ticket and finding out there's a hidden "convenience fee" that costs as much as the ticket itself—not cool, right? Some platforms offer zero-commission trades, like getting a free backstage pass!

Ease of use is vital, especially for beginners. You should avoid attempting spaceship piloting during your first driving lesson, so choose a straightforward navigation platform. Opt for platforms that provide clear instructions, helpful tutorials, and a clean interface. It's akin to having a GPS in your car, ensuring a confusion-free ride.

Research tools and educational resources act as valuable companions on your investment journey, akin to having a knowledgeable roadie who navigates the intricacies of a concert venue. The more knowledge you gain, the sharper your investment choices become.

Lastly, customer service is crucial. If something goes wrong, you want to be sure someone's there to help, just like you'd wish security to be there if someone tried to steal your concert merch.

Remember, choosing the right brokerage platform is like picking the perfect concert outfit—it should be comfortable, suit your style, and make you feel confident.

Understanding Stock Quotes and Market Data

Have you ever wondered how to decode the secret language of stock quotes and market data? Understanding these can be like unlocking a treasure chest of investment wisdom. Let's dive into the meanings of significant stock market indicators and discover how to interpret them like pros, with a tour of the most remarkable internet resources to keep you ahead!

What Are the Major Stock Market Indicators?

Let's explore the fascinating realm of stock market indicators. These instruments serve as your financial detectives, unveiling insights into the unpredictable journey of the stock market. Think of them as your trusted allies, deciphering clues about the market's future direction.

- **Trend Indicators:** Consider these as the market's compass, pointing out its direction. A popular one is the Moving Average. It's like taking a bunch of stock prices over a set period, say 50 days, and averaging them out. This smoothens those daily ups and downs, giving you a more apparent trend line. Another cool one is the Parabolic Stop and Reverse (Parabolic SAR), perfect for spotting potential U-turns in the market price direction.

- **Momentum Indicators:** These are like the market's speedometer, showing how fast prices are moving. The Stochastic Oscillator, for example, helps predict when the market might change direction by comparing the current price to its recent range.

- **Volume Indicators:** Think of these instruments as the market's heartbeat. They gauge the strength of a trend by scrutinizing the volume of shares traded. For instance, let's look at the Chaikin Oscillator—it evaluates the movement of funds in and out of the market, giving us hints about possible market peaks and troughs.

- **Volatility Indicators:** The market's mood rings show how wildly stock prices swing. Bollinger Bands measure the "highness" or "lowness" of price compared to previous trades. If a stock price jumps outside these bands, it's like saying, "Hey, I'm not behaving as usual!"

- **Market Breadth Indicators:** These indicators are popularity contests in the stock market, revealing the level of participation in a trend by counting the number of stocks moving up versus those moving down. A prime illustration is the Advance-Decline Line, which measures the contrast between the stocks on the rise and those on the decline.

- **Market Sentiment Indicators:** These tools act like fortune-tellers for the market, giving insights into whether the mood is bullish (positive) or bearish (negative). The CBOE Volatility Index (VIX), often called the *fear gauge*, gains fame when investors anticipate a market downturn.

Remember that these indicators don't predict the future; they're akin to puzzle pieces that, when assembled, provide a better understanding of the market's sentiment.

Examples in Practice for Interpreting Stock Quotations

Deciphering stock quotes might seem like cracking a code, but it's surprisingly simple once you grasp the key elements. Consider it your insider's guide to evaluating a company's soundness and opportunities. Are you eager to start? Here's your road map to becoming a stock-savvy teenager effortlessly!

- **Bid and Ask:** Think of it this way: The bid is like a buyer's offer when selling a cool sneaker, and the ask is your set price, just like the price tag on the sneaker.

- **Today's Change and Previous Close:** These show how the stock's price has changed compared to yesterday. It's like checking the score change during a basketball game compared to the last game's final score.

- **Volume:** This indicates the number of traded shares at present. When the volume is high, it's like measuring the excitement around a viral video with many people talking about it.

- **52-Week High/Low:** These represent the peak and trough prices over the last year, akin to monitoring your beloved YouTube channel's highest and lowest viewership days.

- **Market Cap:** Market capitalization represents the combined worth of a company's shares. A larger market cap typically indicates a well-established company, akin to comparing a tech giant with a newly launched start-up.

- **P/E Ratio:** Price-Earnings Ratio helps you gauge if a stock is overvalued or undervalued compared to its earnings. It's like comparing the price of a game console to how many fantastic games it offers.

- **Beta:** Beta quantifies a stock's price fluctuations relative to the market. A high beta implies greater risk but the chance for more significant gains, akin to opting for a thrilling rollercoaster instead of a gentle merry-go-round.

- **Dividends:** Some companies pay profits to shareholders. It's like getting a small reward for owning a piece of the company.

Numerous factors can sway stock prices, from corporate updates to worldwide developments. It's akin to staying engaged in an exciting narrative with an ever-evolving storyline. You'll steer through the stock market with expertise by monitoring these crucial elements.

Internet Resources for Monitoring Market Data

Thanks to the quantity of online resources, keeping tabs on stock market information has become more convenient than ever. Tools and websites cater to all, whether you're a novice or an experienced teen investor. Let's discuss the selection of high-quality resources for monitoring stock market data.

- **TIKR:** TIKR is perfect for investors who crave in-depth financial information, boasting comprehensive analyst estimates and worldwide stock data via S&P. Nevertheless, its free version offers restricted functionalities, making it unsuitable for dedicated investors.

- **Stock Rover:** Stock Rover offers robust capabilities for analyzing North American stocks, ETFs, and funds with comprehensive coverage and advanced analytics. Nonetheless, its interface might appear outdated, providing limited information on international stocks.

- **Koyfin:** This highly customizable platform offers advanced graphing and charting capabilities. It's suitable for professional and individual investors but be prepared for a steep learning curve if you're new to using advanced financial tools.

- **Seeking Alpha:** A popular choice for investors of all types, Seeking Alpha provides access to a wide range of stock analysis, real-time market updates, newsletters, and much more. It's a great place for engaging with broad investment research.

- **TradingView:** Known for its extensive charting tools, TradingView is especially popular among more experienced traders. It incorporates social networking functionality and investor education but can be overwhelming for beginners due to its breadth of tools.

- **Finviz:** This intuitive website is excellent for quick stock market checks and fundamental research data. Finviz offers plenty of free market data, including top stock lists, market heatmaps, and news from sources like MarketWatch and Bloomberg.

- **Benzinga Pro:** This platform stands out thanks to its live news updates and features like a stock screener, corporate earnings calendar, and visualization tools. It proves valuable for traders seeking swift trading signals and up-to-the-minute stock updates.

- **Motley Fool:** Known for its in-depth market research and high-quality analysis, Motley Fool provides bi-weekly stock recommendations and has services like Motley Fool Stock Advisor and Rule Breakers, which have historically performed better than the S&P 500.

Each of these platforms possesses its own set of strengths and weaknesses. When selecting the appropriate tool, it's essential to consider your investment approach, experience level, and financial resources. Although these tools offer valuable information, conducting thorough research and weighing all investment choices is essential.

Diversifying Investments Beyond Individual Stocks

Are you prepared to take your investment strategy to the next level, moving beyond stocks? Let's delve into the thrilling universe of ETFs, mutual funds, and other possibilities! We'll examine the risk and return factors, and I'll guide you on crafting a diverse portfolio as distinctive as your cherished playlist.

Other Investing Alternatives

Let's explore some fantastic choices, such as mutual funds and ETFs. Remember, investing isn't only for Wall Street professionals; it's available to everyone, including you!

First, let's talk about mutual funds. Picture them as a blockbuster movie featuring a star-studded ensemble. Each actor represents a stock or bond in this scenario, and their combined performance determines the fund's success. Skilled professionals oversee these funds, and they take charge of the significant decisions, sparing you from worrying about the nitty-gritty details.

Let's dive into exchange-traded funds (ETFs). Think of them as the cool, modern cousins of mutual funds. You can actively trade them on stock exchanges, just like company stocks. They offer great flexibility since you can buy or sell them during trading hours. And the icing on the cake? They frequently come with lower fees than mutual funds, making them an intelligent choice!

Are you familiar with index funds? They mimic a distinct market component, such as the S&P 500. What's excellent about index funds is that they provide diversification and usually come with lower fees. They offer a relaxed approach to riding the market's ups and downs.

Bond funds offer an alternative avenue. They involve loaning money to corporations or governments, yielding interest payments. It's a more relaxed approach and typically less risky compared to stocks.

For the adventurous souls, there's sector and international funds. Sector funds focus on specific industries (like tech or healthcare), while global funds let you globetrot, investing in companies outside your home country. It's like adding some exotic spices to your investment recipe!

Keep in mind that investing isn't a universal solution. What might be suitable for your friend may not apply to you. It's about discovering the perfect blend that matches your style and objectives. Remember that past performance doesn't ensure future results.

Whether you're into the set-it-and-forget-it style of mutual funds or the DIY vibe of ETFs, there's something for everyone in the investment universe. Dive in and explore, and you might be the next investment guru among your friends!

Risk and Return of Investment Vehicles

Let's dive into the exciting world of investment vehicles. Think of these as different types of cars on your journey to financial success—each has its speed, comfort level, and destination. Ready to explore?

- **Stocks—The Speedy Sports Cars:** Owning stocks is akin to possessing a company part. When the company thrives, your shares appreciate, and some even provide dividends. However, it's a rollercoaster journey! Stocks can soar or plummet, contingent on the company and market circumstances. They suit individuals comfortable with such volatility.

- **Bonds—The Reliable Sedans:** Think of bonds as a way to loan your money to a government or company. In return, they pay you interest. Bonds are like the dependable sedans of investments—not as thrilling as sports cars (stocks) but far less prone to unexpected issues.

- **Mutual Funds—The Versatile SUVs:** Professionally managed, these funds gather investments from multiple people to purchase various assets like stocks and bonds. They provide diversification, spreading your risk across different investment types, similar to having an all-terrain SUV.

- **ETFs (Exchange-Traded Funds)—The Modern Hybrids:** ETFs, like mutual funds, operate on stock exchanges but mimic index performance, such as the S&P 500. They provide a mix of safety and growth, akin to a versatile hybrid car, making them a suitable choice for many investors.

- **Real Estate Investment Trusts (REITs)—The Sturdy Pickup Trucks:** REITs offer a way to invest in real estate without direct ownership. Instead, they oversee real estate, boosting property value and rental income. Imagine having a fleet of dependable pickup trucks handling the hard work on your behalf.

- **Cryptocurrencies—The Exotic Supercars:** They're new, fast, and sometimes unpredictable. Investing in cryptocurrencies like Bitcoin can lead to high returns, but remember that they're risky. They can be subject to wild price changes and are only for those ready for a thrilling but potentially risky ride.

- **Fine Art and Wine—The Classic Vintage Cars:** These are not your everyday investments but can be rewarding. Art and wine increase in value over time, but they require knowledge, patience, and a bit of flair. Think of them as classic vintage cars—they might not be for everyday use, but they can be a showstopper if you know what you're doing.

- **Cash and Savings—The Trusty Bicycles:** Cash investments like savings accounts and CDs are safe but offer low returns. They're like bicycles—not fast or glamorous, but they'll get you where you need to go without breaking down.

Choosing a suitable investment relies on your objectives, how much risk you can take, and how long you intend to invest. Just as new drivers learn about different types of vehicles, young investors should understand each investment category before putting their money in. And don't forget the value of diversification—don't put all your funds in one investment!

Before venturing on your investment journey, performing a thorough analysis is essential. Just as you would purchase a car only if you do your homework, ensure that you invest with a clear understanding of what you're entering.

Tips on Creating a Portfolio of Varied Investments

Creating a diverse investment portfolio is a crucial step toward financial security and growth, especially for you, the savvy teens of today! Imagine your portfolio as a superhero team—each member brings unique strengths, balancing each other out. Now, let's dive into how you can assemble your financial Avengers.

- **Understand Your Unique Superpowers (Risk Tolerance and Goals):** Just like every superhero has his or her strengths and weaknesses, your investment choices should align with your personal risk tolerance and financial goals. If you're a daredevil, ready to take on high-risk, high-reward missions, stocks might be your thing. But if you're more of the cautious sidekick, bonds could be your ally. Remember, your goals matter, too. Saving for a car in a few years? That's a different game than prepping for retirement decades away.

- **Assemble Your Team (Diverse Assets):** Building a diverse team is essential. Although stocks and bonds are a powerful pair in investing, they aren't the whole story. Introduce real estate (via REITs), commodities, and international stocks to your crew. It's akin to assembling a team with varied strengths—when one falters, the others can step in. Diversification acts as your defense against market ups and downs. For instance, while tech stocks surge, real estate can offer dependable rental income.

- **Stay Informed and Adapt (Regular Portfolio Review):** Like superheroes adjust their strategies, regularly reviewing and rebalancing your portfolio is essential. The market changes and so should your investments. If one part of your portfolio starts taking over (like if tech stocks suddenly make up 70% of your investments), it's time to rebalance. Think of it as keeping your team in harmony.

- **The Power of Compounding (Start Early):** Your superpower lies in starting early because compounding interest allows even modest, consistent investments to multiply into substantial wealth over time. It's akin to honing your super abilities—the more you practice, the mightier you become.

- **Beware of Villains (Avoid Common Mistakes):** Just like every superhero faces challenges, there are pitfalls to avoid in investing. Don't put all your eggs in one basket (overconcentration), don't panic when the market dips (emotional investing), and don't ignore the costs (like high fund fees).

Always keep in mind that building a diversified investment portfolio is a strategy. Begin with modest steps, maintain a steady approach, and continue to grow your knowledge. Your investment tactics will also develop as you gain experience and wisdom.

Key Takeaways

- To open a brokerage account, choose a reputable brokerage, gather essential documents, and fill out an online application.

- There are various accounts for teens, including custodial accounts, individual accounts, education accounts, and retirement accounts.

- When selecting a brokerage platform, prioritize trustworthiness, low fees, user-friendliness, research tools, and customer service.

- Stock quotes and market data are like a secret language. Understanding bid, ask, volume and other indicators helps you make informed decisions.

- Key indicators include trend indicators, momentum indicators, volume indicators, volatility indicators, market breadth indicators, and market sentiment indicators.

- Beyond individual stocks, explore mutual funds, ETFs, index funds, bond funds, sector funds, international funds, and retirement accounts.

- Building a diversified portfolio involves understanding your risk tolerance, assembling diverse assets, regularly reviewing and rebalancing, leveraging compounding, and avoiding common investment mistakes.

- Start early, stay consistent, and consider seeking advice from financial experts or using robo-advisors as you grow in your investment journey.

Now that you've embarked on your journey to conquer the stock market, let's level up your strategic decision-making skills! We've covered opening your first brokerage account, decoding stock quotes, and diversifying beyond individual stocks. It's time to become the mastermind of your financial adventure!

Chapter 3:

Strategic Stock Market Decision-Making

Do you believe you can outsmart the stock market? Get ready for a wild ride! Trying to time the market is as complex as navigating through a Greek myth, with more legends than truths. Some claim they have it all figured out; but realistically, it's a tough nut to crack. We all make mistakes occasionally, and in the stock market, a tiny slip-up can lead to considerable losses. So, let's explore the dos and don'ts of investing. Get ready to buckle up as we uncover and steer clear of the blunders that even experienced pros can fall into!

Strategic Stock Market Decision-Making

Let's set off on an adventure into the realms of fundamental and technical analysis. Imagine this as your treasure-hunting kit for discovering the stock market's hidden jewels. Like a detective unraveling clues, we will explore and evaluate different stocks together. But here, you're uncovering exciting investment chances!

Introduction to Fundamental and Technical Analysis

Buckle up because we're about to explore two fantastic ways to analyze stocks: fundamental and technical analysis. These aren't just dull old methods; they're your secret weapons in understanding and conquering the stock market!

Let's kick off with **fundamental analysis**—it's like playing detective. You'll delve into a company's financials and economic indicators, assessing its value and growth potential. Imagine sizing up a book by its content, not just the cover. Take the price-to-earnings (P/E) ratio, for instance; it clues you in on whether a stock is an undiscovered treasure (undervalued) or a bit overpriced (overvalued).

Let's pivot to **technical analysis**, akin to playing meteorologist for the stock market. Here, you dive into scrutinizing market data, focusing on price and volume charts, to identify trends and forecast future movements. The spotlight isn't on the company's activities but on its stock's performance. Utilizing tools like trend lines, you'll get a clearer picture of the stock's potential future direction.

But here's the twist: These two methods are like chocolate and peanut butter—great on their own but even better together! Some savvy investors use fundamental analysis to pick a stock and technical analysis to decide when to buy or sell it. It's like finding a fabulous pair of sneakers at a great price and then waiting for the perfect moment to rock them.

Some folks argue about which method is better. But, hey, why not use both? Each has its strengths, and combining them can give you a fuller picture of where to invest your hard-earned cash.

How to Investigate and Evaluate Various Stocks

Let's embark on an exciting journey into stock market research, like a thrilling treasure hunt! Instead of seeking gold coins, we're after intelligent investment decisions. This quick guide will turn you into a clever stock detective, ready to uncover hidden investment gems!

- **Gather Your Detective Tools:** Like any good detective, you need your tools. In stock research, this means diving into a company's financials. Start with their annual and quarterly reports (Form 10-K and 10-Q) on the SEC's EDGAR database. These reports are like a company's diary, telling you about their money matters, from how much they earn (revenue) to what they have left after paying bills (net income).

- **Focus on the Clues:** In the sea of numbers, focus on key terms like earnings per share (EPS) and price-earnings ratio (P/E). EPS shows how much profit a company makes for each share, while P/E tells you how much investors will shell out for every dollar of the company's earnings. Think of EPS as the company's report card and P/E as its popularity score with investors.

- **The Story Behind the Numbers:** Numbers only tell part of the story. Now, think about the company's plot: What do they do? Who leads them? Who are their competitors? This is like understanding the character and setting of a story to predict the following chapters.

- **Different Ways to Solve the Mystery:** There are two main detective approaches: fundamental analysis, which looks at the company's value based on its actual business performance and financial health, and technical analysis, like reading tea leaves but for stock charts. It looks for patterns in stock prices to predict future movements.

Selecting stocks can feel like a gamble, like rooting for your favorite sports team. They might win or lose, but that's just the nature of the game. Remember, never invest everything in one place. Spread your investments to diversify and reduce risk.

Stock research can be as exciting as a mystery novel, with profits as the prize for your detective skills. Dive in and stay curious, and you might find your treasure!

Advice for Assessing Investment Prospects

First, let's talk about your game plan for investing in stocks. Imagine you're at a buffet—you don't just grab everything, right? Similarly, investing is about picking the right stocks that suit your taste (financial goals). Remember, about 51% of Americans plan to invest outside retirement accounts this year and 60% in tax-advantaged investments (Marder, 2023). Pretty cool, right? So, you're not alone in this adventure.

Now, let's get real—stocks are like rollercoasters. Think about it: If everyone expects big things and they don't happen, that's a bummer, right? So, balance your expectations and look into value-style stocks like financials, industrials, utilities, and healthcare.

Hoping the United States avoids a recession (let's keep our fingers crossed!), sectors such as materials, industrials, and consumer discretionary might spearhead the growth. However, if a recession sneaks in, you might find shelter in defensive sectors like healthcare, utilities, and consumer staples.

Also, remember the cash problem. While cash has its perks, it might not be the superstar in the coming year, especially with interest rates expected to drop. So, think about how money fits into your master plan.

Bonds are making a comeback, providing a comfortable blend of stability, income, and the chance for prices to rise. Don't rely solely on my advice; take the time to research and find what aligns with your financial objectives.

Timing the Market: Myths and Realities

Picture the intriguing world of market timing as a daring quest to catch the ultimate surfing wave—a captivating analogy, right? But here's the twist: Mastering market timing involves debunking widespread misconceptions and facing some cold, complex realities. It's like predicting the twists and turns of the world's most unpredictable rollercoaster. Additionally, we'll underscore the importance of embracing a long-term outlook in your investments. So, snatch your financial surfboard, and let's conquer the stock market's challenges as a team!

Common Misconceptions About Market Timing Busted

Let's bust some myths about market timing in stock investing in a fun, informative way, especially for you, the savvy teenagers ready to take on the investing world!

- **You Need a Crystal Ball to Time the Market:** Nope! Timing the market isn't about predicting the exact top and bottom. It's more about understanding the broader trends and making educated decisions. Think of it like trying to catch a wave when surfing: You don't need to see the giant wave; you can ride one smoothly.

- **Only the Rich Can Play the Stock Market Game:** Forget the old days when only the rich could play the investment game. Nowadays, with tools like discount brokers and fractional shares, even those with just a bit of cash can jump into investing. It's like a video game level-up: Begin modestly, master the basics, and gradually expand your investments.

- **You Must Glue Your Eyes to the Market 24-7:** Take it easy! Successful investing isn't about responding to every market twitch. It's more about a solid long-term plan and patience. Think of it as planting a tree: You don't keep checking its growth daily—just let it grow over time!

- **More Risk = More Money:** Diving into investing involves some risk-taking, but remember, jumping in blindfolded can send you tumbling down a risky slope. The key is striking the perfect balance that aligns with your goals and how much uncertainty you can handle comfortably.

- **Professional Traders Always Win:** Surprisingly, professionals don't consistently excel in this area. Studies indicate that actively managed funds frequently fall short of passive index funds in the long run. This suggests that becoming a Wall Street expert is optional for achieving investment success.

- **Timing the Market Is Everything:** Here's a fun twist: Success in the stock market is more about the time spent *in* the market, not trying to time it perfectly. Think of it as sticking to your investment plan through thick and thin, just like committing to your workout routine to achieve that summer body!

- **All Stocks Are Equally Risky:** Like in a video game, stocks come with different levels of risk. Some paths are safer and more predictable, offering a steady journey. Others, though riskier, can lead to faster gains, providing a more exciting adventure. Your choice depends on your preferred playstyle!

- **I'm Too Late to Start Investing:** Starting your investment journey is always timely, no matter your life stage. Picture it like arriving at a party—whether you're early or a bit late, the fun is always there for the taking.

- **Get Rich Quick in the Stock Market:** Hold your horses! The stock market isn't a lottery ticket. It's about building wealth gradually. Chasing quick riches is like sprinting at the start of a marathon; you'll likely burn out fast.

- **Only Invest in Stocks and You're Set:** Maintain well-rounded financial health by mixing stocks, bonds, and real estate in your portfolio. Just like a balanced diet, diversity is the key to success!

- **Past Performance Guarantees Future Results:** Remember, past performance is like last year's sports scores—exciting but not a sure bet for future games.

- **You Need to Be a Financial Guru:** No need to be a finance guru to dive into investing. It's all about grasping the essentials and making intelligent decisions. Imagine it's like picking up a new game—begin with the simple rules and you'll soon master it.

Investing isn't some mysterious craft; it's a skill you can sharpen through understanding, patience, and strategic planning. Remember that a slow and steady approach often leads to victory, even in the stock market.

Problems Involved in Trying to Time the Market

Timing the market, or attempting to predict its highs and lows for investment purposes, is a notoriously tricky task, and recent research supports this. Here's a light-hearted but informative take on why you, as a teenager, might want to think twice before trying to outsmart the market:

- **It's Like Trying to Catch a Falling Knife:** Grasping a falling knife without getting hurt is as challenging as predicting the market's perfect moment. According to the Schwab Center for Financial Research findings, they made a fascinating discovery. Over 20 years, they examined five different investment approaches and observed that an investor who acted promptly lagged behind an expert market timer by just around $10,000 after two decades (*Does Market Timing Work?* 2023).

- **The Tortoise Beats the Hare:** In investing, just like the story of the tortoise and the hare, the slow and steady approach often comes out on top. Quick riches can tempt you into hasty choices, but patience and discipline pay off. Choosing stable companies for long-term investments brings better rewards than following every fleeting trend in the stock market.

- **Not Even the Pros Can Do It Consistently:** Are you aspiring to be the next Warren Buffett? Keep in mind that even seasoned experts need help with mastering market timing. Both professional and individual investors often need more discipline to match the market's performance in the long run, primarily due to impatience or a lack of discipline. Buffett's counsel is straightforward: "You pay for the price, but you receive value." So, it's wiser to focus on the worth of reliable companies rather than chasing the ideal times to buy and sell (Waldron, 2023).

- **The Crystal Ball Is Cloudy:** Predicting the market resembles deciphering a foggy crystal ball packed with countless variables and uncertainties. Successful market timing usually hinges more on luck than expertise. Remember this sage advice: Your duration in the market, rather than trying to time it, truly matters.

Like trying to beat a video game on the hardest difficulty, timing the market is challenging; even the best players often fail. It's more about setting up a consistent strategy, being patient, and focusing on the long-term game rather than trying to make the perfect move at the ideal time. Stay calm, invest wisely, and remember that even the tortoise reached the finish line!

Importance of Having a Lengthy Investment Perspective

First, did you know that 75% of teens believe investing is essential, but only about 23% have started doing it? Yep, that's according to Fidelity's 2023 Teens & Money Study (*Fidelity Study Reveals Teens Think Investing Is Important*, 2023). And here's another fun fact: About half of Americans plan to invest outside their retirement accounts in 2024 (Marder, 2023). So, it's not just you thinking about growing that cash stash!

Imagine investing today and witnessing your money expand exponentially over time, thanks to the wonder of compound growth. It's like nurturing a tiny seed that eventually blossoms into a massive tree. When you start investing as a teenager, your money has more time to grow exponentially, showing you the power of patience and the multiplying effect of compounding.

Investing isn't only for adults anymore! Fidelity has stepped up the game by launching an app designed for teens to dive into the investing world. It's super cool! With this app, you can start trading mutual funds, stocks, and ETFs, and guess what? You can begin your investment journey with just $1 (*Fidelity Study Reveals Teens Think Investing Is Important*, 2023).

Remember, investing isn't just a shortcut to cash. It's the key to establishing a solid base for your future goals, whether college, a shiny new car, or that dream vacation. By getting started early, you save money and sow the seeds for a prosperous future. Take that first step, and watch your finances bloom!

Typical Investing Mistakes to Avoid

Starting your investment adventure is like hopping on a rollercoaster—exciting but bumpy, especially at the beginning. Have you ever heard about those "whoops" moments even seasoned investors had in their early days? They've walked that path. Diving into decisions without proper research or mindlessly following the crowd? Those are big investment faux pas to steer clear of.

Common Mistakes Inexperienced Investors Make

Investing holds great promise for young investors like yourself, offering excitement and potential rewards. However, like any journey, it has its share of traps to sidestep. Below, we'll explore typical blunders new investors often encounter and guide you on how to steer clear of them. Keep in mind that even the investment legends began their journeys as beginners!

- **Chasing Performance:** It's like going after the popular crowd at school, thinking they'll always be on top. In the investing world, just because a stock or fund has done well recently doesn't mean it will continue to do so. A startling statistic shows that out of 549 top-performing equity funds in 2017, less than 3% stayed in the top four years later (Prince, 2022). So, it's about grasping the long-term potential, not simply chasing what's trendy.

- **Hindsight Bias:** Have you ever caught yourself thinking, *I saw that coming!* after something happens? That's what we call hindsight bias. It's a sneaky trap in investing, where you might join the crowd rushing into hot investments only to realize you're late to the party. Picture this: Investors flocking to equity funds in 1999, just as the tech bubble popped, or folks piling up on bonds and missing out on the bull market after the crisis. It's all about timing; sometimes, it's not on our side! (Prince, 2022). Investing involves making informed decisions, not forecasting the future based on past events.

- **Not Controlling Emotions:** Investing can be a rollercoaster of excitement and fear, but letting emotions drive your decisions is a no-go. Think of it like choosing your favorite football team—just because you love them doesn't mean they'll win the championship. In investing, this emotional bias can lead to poor choices like selling too soon or not diversifying enough.

- **Failing to Diversify:** Wise investing is akin to having a diverse group of friends. Relying on just one friend wouldn't be your go-to choice. Likewise, concentrating all your funds on a single asset or market carries risks. Through diversification, you distribute your investments across different types of assets, markets, and timeframes, creating a more secure financial circle of friends.

- **Sitting Out During Bear Markets:** It's tempting to avoid investing when the market looks scary, like not wanting to play a game you think you'll lose. However, preventing the market can mean missing out on good opportunities. Remember, the market often starts recovering before the economy does, so there's potential for gains even in tough times.

- **Investing in the Unknown:** Just like you would only join a club if you know what it's about, don't invest in businesses you don't understand. Unfamiliarity can lead to poor decision-making and, ultimately, losses. Take the time to research and comprehend a company before investing your hard-earned money.

Like any skill, investing improves with practice and learning from others' mistakes. Continuously refine your strategy, stay informed, diversify your investments, and maintain emotional control during decision-making. Remember that investing is a long journey, not a quick race. The intelligent decisions you make now will benefit your future self!

How to Prevent Making Hasty Decisions

Let's talk about avoiding hasty decisions in stock investing—a crucial skill for navigating the rollercoaster world of finance. Remember, this isn't a sprint; it's more like a strategic chess game.

- **Understand That Markets Recover:** You know how there's a rainbow after every storm? Stock markets are similar. They have ups and downs, but history shows they always bounce back. Even after significant events like the Global Financial Crisis or the COVID-19 pandemic, markets recovered and often reached new highs (Wise, 2023). So, don't freak out with every dip!

- **Have a Plan and Stick to It:** Picture setting off on a road trip without a map—a bit daunting. That's like investing without a clear strategy. Establish your investment objectives, understand risk tolerance, and build a varied portfolio. Doing this makes it easier to remain composed during market ups and downs and avoid impulsive decisions.

- **Diversification Is Your Best Friend:** Avoid putting all your investments in the same spot. Diversify across various sectors, asset classes, and regions. By doing this, if a single industry or area faces trouble, your entire investment portfolio won't tumble. It's like setting up a safety net for your finances.

- **Check Your Emotions at the Door:** Warren Buffett, often dubbed the LeBron James of investing, emphasizes that success in investing isn't solely dependent on a high IQ. Instead, it's about mastering your emotions. Making impulsive decisions during market downturns, like hastily withdrawing your investments, can often result in regret when the market eventually rebounds.

- **Learn From Practice, Not Just Theory:** Before diving into the real deal, why not try paper trading? It's like playing a stock market video game with fake money. This helps you understand market trends and build confidence before investing in real cash.

- **Beware of the Herd Mentality:** Have you ever mindlessly followed your friends and wondered, *Why did I go along with that?* Well, the same can happen when it comes to investing. What might have worked for someone else must align with your financial objectives. Steer clear of hopping on the trend of the latest buzzworthy stock that everyone's raving about.

- **Stay Informed, Not Influenced:** Amidst the deluge of information today, it's simple to be influenced by the newest updates or social media hype. Remember that your investment choices should stem from thorough research and be in sync with your long-term objectives, not merely following what's trending on X (formerly Twitter).

- **Keep a Diary—Yes, Seriously:** Writing down your investment decisions and their reasons can be super helpful. It's like keeping a diary, but you're tracking your financial moves instead of your secret crushes. This can be an excellent tool for reflecting on your decisions and improving over time.

Think of investing like tending to a tree. It requires time, patience, and creating the perfect environment for growth. Rushing can lead to mistakes, but you can watch your investments flourish consistently by following a thoughtful strategy. Stay determined, keep learning, and remember that the journey is as important as the destination.

Insights From Past Occurrences in the Industry

First, remember that stock market history is a treasure trove of wisdom. Let's time-travel back to 2015–2022. During these years, investors grappled with wild rides like the 2015 manufacturing recession, the 2020 global pandemic recession, Brexit, and more. For instance, the NASDAQ had a heart-stopping 23% sell-off in 2018—yikes (Ryniec, 2022)! However, those who clung to their seats with a solid investing plan were the real MVPs.

Now, let's talk about the big players. Take ExxonMobil (XOM), for example. After crude oil prices crashed in 2014–2015, its stocks seemed like a steal. But, plot twist! The expected recovery was a no-show, and its shares underperformed for years. However, they bounced back in 2021, hitting a new two-year high (Ryniec, 2022). The lesson? Patience and timing are everything.

Then there's JPMorgan Chase (JPM). Post-financial crisis, its shares yo-yoed, but it seemed like a green light when CEO Jamie Dimon bought $25 million of its stock. The catch? The industry didn't explode as expected. Yet, JPMorgan Chase's shares saw a 67% gain during the pandemic (Ryniec, 2022). Here's the takeaway: Even industry giants have their ups and downs.

Don't forget NVIDIA (NVDA). In 2017, semiconductor stocks, including NVIDIA, skyrocketed (Ryniec, 2022). Although NVIDIA had its moments of weakness, it remained a hot pick for investors. The key here? Keeping an eye on industry trends can pay off big time.

Lastly, PayPal (PYPL). In the past seven years, PayPal's shares soared by 367%, outperforming the Nasdaq. But then came a steep drop (Ryniec, 2022). The lesson? High-flying stocks can be tricky; they can climb to dizzying heights and then suddenly nosedive.

Stock investing is like navigating a maze with hidden treasures. It's not just about picking stocks; it's about understanding the market's ebbs and flows, learning from past mistakes, and having a clear strategy.

Key Takeaways

- Timing the market is tricky, more myth than reality, so focus on long-term strategies instead of trying to predict the perfect moment.

- Avoid common newbie mistakes: chasing hot stocks, letting emotions rule, and putting all your eggs in one basket.

- Stay cool during market dips. History shows markets bounce back, so think long-term and don't panic.

- Blend diversification into your strategy. Distribute your investments across various sectors and asset classes to create a safety cushion.

- Don't just follow the herd. Make investment choices matching your goals and risk appetite.

- When making decisions, stay level-headed and rely on research and strategy, not just market hype or fear.

- Remember, the stock market's history is a treasure trove of lessons about patience, timing, and staying calm under pressure.

Now that we've navigated the stock market's tricky waters, let's dive into the exciting world of investment risk awareness and mitigation. Think of it like learning to surf—you've got to know the waves to ride them safely. Ready to catch the next big wave?

Chapter 4:

Investment Risk Awareness and Mitigation

Get ready for an incredible journey into intelligent investing! First, we will navigate through investment risk awareness and mitigation—consider it your money armor, shielding you from those sneaky market surprises. Then, we'll jump into building long-term wealth, like nurturing a fantastic money tree that flourishes as time goes by. Lastly, we'll ace the game of setting financial goals and milestones, plotting your epic quest for stock market treasure.

Investment Risk Awareness and Mitigation

Knowing the ropes of investment risk and how to dodge those sneaky pitfalls is crucial. So, grab your financial adventure gear, and let's dive into the exciting world of risk awareness and intelligent moves in stock investing!

Categories of Investing Hazards

Buckle up because we're about to explore the different types of investment risks that you might encounter. Think of it as a rollercoaster ride in the financial world!

- **Lingering Inflation:** Picture this: Prices for your favorite snacks keep increasing, but your weekly allowance doesn't. That's inflation for you, and it can be a real party pooper for your investments, too. Inflation can eat into the actual value of your returns significantly if your investments aren't growing fast enough to outpace it.

- **Rate Hikes Offsetting Rate Cuts:** Imagine you're saving up for a new game, and suddenly, the price fluctuates wildly. Annoying, right? That's similar to what happens in the investment world with interest rates. Changes in interest rates can make the market go up and down, affecting everything from bond prices to how much companies can borrow.

- **AI and Tech Trends:** Just like everyone's talking about the latest video game, investors get hyped about tech trends like artificial intelligence (AI). But here's the catch: If these trends don't live up to the hype, it can lead to losses for those who invested heavily in them.

- **Credit Stress in Certain Sectors:** Consider this a school project where some team members struggle. Some sectors face tough times in the investment world, making it harder to pay back their debts. This can be a risk, primarily if you've invested in those sectors.

- **Diverse Investment Options and Their Risks:** Investment options are as varied as your playlist. You've got the chill vibes of savings accounts and government bonds—low risk but with modest returns, like cruising on a bike. Then, there are the more daring choices like stocks and mutual funds. They're like skateboarding down a steep hill—riskier but with the potential for a bigger adrenaline rush (and returns!). Each choice has its blend of excitement and hazards.

Investing is similar to picking a path in a video game—you'll find that some choices carry more risk, but they might also bring more significant rewards. It's all about playing it smart, knowing the risks, and making clever decisions. So, as you dive into the investing game, remember to weigh these risks and see how they fit with what you're aiming for.

Risk Management and Mitigation Techniques

First, the stock market can be like a rollercoaster—exciting but sometimes scary. Here's how you can buckle up and enjoy the ride while keeping the risks at bay:

- **Mix It Up (Diversification):** Consider investments like your music playlist. You wouldn't want just one kind of song. It's the same with stocks. Mix it up! Stocks, bonds, and maybe some cash. This way, if one type goes down, the others stay steady or even go up.

- **Stay Steady (Dollar-Cost Averaging):** Think about picking up your go-to snack every time you hit the store, whether it's on sale or a bit pricey. This is just like dollar-cost averaging in investing. Here, you're putting in a consistent amount of cash regularly. When investment prices dip, your set amount snags more shares; when prices rise, you get fewer. This strategy is an incredible way to steadily grow your investment stash, sidestepping the tricky game of guessing the market's next move.

- **Know Your Comfort Zone (Risk Tolerance):** Are you the bungee-jumping type or more of a chill-on-the-beach person? Figuring out your comfort level with risk is vital when picking stocks. If you're all about keeping cool, steer toward safer investment options. But hey, if you're up for a thrill, dive into stocks that promise higher rewards but also come with their share of rollercoaster rides!

- **Homework Time (Fundamental Analysis):** Doing your homework is critical! Before you invest in a company, snoop around its financials. Peep their assets, debts, and how much dough they're making. It's like creeping into a company's social media profile before you slide into their investment DMs. Always know what you're getting into!

- **Play Detective (Technical Analysis):** It's similar to forecasting tomorrow's weather based on today's—you use charts and patterns to make educated guesses about future stock prices. No, it's not magic, but it's a terrific method for creating intelligent predictions!

- **Safety Nets (Stop-Loss Orders):** Imagine a safety net catching you if you fall. Stop-loss orders are like that. They automatically sell your stock if its price drops to a certain level, preventing more significant losses. It's like having a backup plan.

- **Regular Check-Ups (Portfolio Reviews):** Just like you're constantly scrolling through your social media, remember to give your investments some screen time too! It's all about ensuring they're still on track with your objectives. If your goals have shifted or the markets have done a one-eighty, tweak your game plan accordingly. Stay sharp and keep your investments as updated as your Insta stories!

- **The Slow and Steady Wins (Value Investing):** Imagine discovering a super cool band that's not yet famous but has mega-hit potential. That's what value investing is all about. You scout for stocks currently under the radar and priced low, but they're like hidden gems waiting to shine and increase in value over the long haul. It's like being ahead of the trend in the stock market!

So, remember, investing isn't just about making quick money. It's about being smart, researching, and playing the long game. And, hey, even if things don't always go as planned, each experience is a step toward becoming a savvy investor.

Importance of Diversification in Risk Management

Imagine you're at a buffet, and instead of piling your plate with just spaghetti (yummy), you add some salad, a bit of chicken, maybe a slice of pizza, and a scoop of ice cream. That's diversification—mixing things up to enjoy a balanced meal. Diversifying means spreading your money across different investments (stocks, bonds, real estate), industries (tech, healthcare, retail), and countries. It's like building a superhero team where each member brings a unique power.

But why is diversification important? The stock market is like a thrilling rollercoaster; if you stash all your cash in a single ride, it can get pretty bumpy. If that one ride goes downhill, it can hurt! That's where diversification steps in as your financial cushion. It's like having a bunch of different rides to enjoy, so even if one has a rough day, you've got others to keep the excitement going. For example, when the 2008 financial crisis hit, folks who had spread their money across various investments did better than those who bet everything on just one.

But here's a twist: In 2023, diversification only worked like a charm for some. Investors who spread their money across various sectors—financials, retailers, and foods—faced a tough time. This shows that diversification isn't a magic shield; it's more like a strategic move in your investment game plan.

Remember, there's no one-size-fits-all strategy. Your investment mix should match your personal goals, timeline, and comfort with risk. You could be a daredevil investor, loving the thrill of high-risk stocks, or a cautious one, preferring the steady ride of bonds. It's all about finding your style and sticking to it.

Adjust your investment mix regularly, like giving your investment vehicle a check-up to ensure it's cruising smoothly and heading in the right direction according to your goals.

Diversifying your investments is crucial in today's unpredictable financial landscape. It's like assembling a team of financial superheroes that have your back. When you diversify your investments, you're like a superhero with a safety net, ready to catch you if the market takes a sudden dip. It's like having your squad of money protectors, ensuring your wealth stays safe and grows over time.

Think of diversification as your ace card in the stock market game. When you play it smart, your investment garden doesn't rely on just one money tree; it's a colorful forest of money trees, each with its treasures.

Creating Long-Term Wealth

Ready to dive into the stock market ocean and fish for long-term wealth? It's not only about quick wins; think of it as growing a money tree. With smart choices and patience, you'll be harvesting big financial fruits before you know it!

How Compound Interest Affects the Growth of Wealth

Imagine compound interest as a turbocharged version of regular interest. It goes beyond earning interest only on your starting amount; it also adds interest on the interest you've already attained. Imagine it as a snowball zooming downhill, getting bigger and mightier with every roll!

Picture this in stock investing: When you own stocks that pay you dividends and put them back into your investment, it's like earning extra money on the money you already gained. And as time goes on, this can make your initial investment grow much more extensive. It's like having a snowball fight where each snowball you toss becomes even more giant in the end!

Imagine this scenario: You decide to invest $1,000 in a stock, and it's on a roll, growing at a solid 7% each year. Fast forward a decade and you'll witness something magical. It's not just your original $1,000 plus a decade's worth of interest; thanks to the compound interest effect, your investment could swell to around $1,967! That's almost like doubling your money without any extra effort!

The more you allow your investments to simmer in the market, the bigger the probable rewards. It's like a game for patient investors; the gains can be satisfying. The secret sauce? Getting in the game early. Investing sooner gives compound interest more time to perform its financial wizardry.

Now, let's sprinkle in some recent findings. According to a 2024 NerdWallet survey, about half of Americans plan to invest outside retirement accounts, with stocks being a popular choice (Marder, 2023). This enthusiasm for stocks among young and older generations underscores the growing understanding and appreciation of compound interest in wealth growth.

But remember, investing in stocks isn't a guaranteed win. The market can be as unpredictable as your Wi-Fi signal. That's why diversifying your investments is crucial. Spread your money across investments like bonds, real estate, or a high-yield savings account for a safer bet.

Compound interest in stock investing acts as your trusty financial sidekick. Get a head start, mix up your investments, and watch the enchanting power of time multiply your wealth. Sooner than you think, you'll be on your journey to financial greatness! Always remember, when it comes to investing, time is your ultimate ally.

Real-World Instances of How the Compounding Effect Works

Let's kick things off with a story about Colgate-Palmolive. Picture this: If you had put $1,000 into Colgate-Palmolive stocks in 1990, fast forward to today and you'd be sitting on a cool $30,502! That's the magic of compound interest, transforming a simple investment into a mini treasure chest over the years.

Here's the excellent strategy: Take those dividends and invest them in more Colgate-Palmolive stocks, riding the wave of their growth, especially in international markets. Their innovative advertisements and worldwide presence have made their stock skyrocket, like leveling up in a game by reinvesting your points!

Imagine this: You invest $1,000 in a stock and it grows by 7% each year. After the first year, your investment becomes $1,070. In the second year, it gains another 7% based on the new amount, which keeps happening. It's like a money snowball rolling down a hill, getting more extensive as it goes—that makes compounding super cool in stocks!

For instance, you're cautious and prefer certificates of deposit (CDs). If you invest $10,000 in a CD with a 5% interest rate, the first year gives you $500 in interest. But here's where it gets cool: The following year, you earn interest on the new total of $10,500, not just the original $10,000. This cycle continues, growing your investment even more.

Tips on How to Use Compound Interest to Achieve Long-Term Financial Goals

Picture compound interest like a snowball zooming down a hill. The longer it rolls, the bigger it gets. It's not just about the interest on your starting cash but also the interest that piles up along the way. Imagine it as making interest on the interest you've already earned. Super cool, right?

Getting a head start is the key here. The sooner you kick off your savings or investments, the more time your money gets to do its thing. Picture this: You put $1,000 into an investment that earns 5% interest each year. Fast forward 20 years and without chipping in any extra cash, you'd be looking at roughly $2,653! That's more than double your initial investment, all thanks to the enchanting power of compound interest.

Reinvesting your earnings (like dividends from stocks or mutual funds) can supercharge this growth. It's like adding more snow to your snowball as it rolls down the hill. This approach can significantly boost your returns over time.

Now, when it comes to maximizing compound interest, kick-start your game plan by establishing well-defined financial objectives. Are you aiming to stash away cash for an epic vacation, your college fund, or that nifty gadget you've been eyeing? Having a crystal-clear target in mind is your secret weapon for staying on track and maintaining your financial discipline.

Now, let's break it down: There are short-term goals that you can conquer in a year or less, such as scoring that new gaming console. Conversely, long-term goals, like squirreling cash for college or a shiny new car, take more time to achieve. And guess what? Compound interest is like a superhero for those long-term goals because it gets more time to do its money-making wizardry!

Check out this superb formula for compound interest: $F = P(1 + r/n)^{\wedge}(nt)$. In this, F stands for what your investment will grow into, P is the cash you start with, r is your yearly interest rate, n is how often the interest gets added yearly, and t is the total years your money's in play. Like a magic spell, huh? It's some nifty math showing how your money can accumulate over time. So, get ready to watch your savings transform into something extraordinary!

Of course, hurdles like inflation and investment fees can slow down your compound interest train. But by choosing investments wisely, diversifying your portfolio, and understanding tax implications, you can keep your train chugging along.

Remember, the key ingredients to compound interest success are time, patience, and regular contributions. It's like planting a tree. The best time was 20 years ago. The second best time is now.

Setting Financial Goals and Milestones

Setting financial goals in stock investing is like starting an epic quest in your favorite game. It's all about plotting your journey to Fortune City, marking milestones like a pro, and having a blast while watching your investments level up. Ready to start your adventure?

Guidance on Setting Short-Term and Long-Term Financial Goals

First, let's start with gaining knowledge. The stock market is a massive puzzle, filled with elements like stocks, bonds, mutual funds, etc. To succeed, you've got to grasp these components just like leveling up in your favorite video game—the more you discover, the sharper your skills become.

Now, onto setting goals. Imagine you want to buy something big in the future, like a car or even a trip to Mars (hey, it could happen!). You need to start saving and investing to make these dreams a reality. But don't just dive in; start small and learn as you go. It's like learning to skateboard—you don't begin with a 360 kickflip on day one, right? Around 23% of teens are already investing, and 91% are eager to start (*2023 Teens and Money Study*, n.d.). So, you're in good company!

Here's a pro tip: Avoid putting all your eggs in one basket. This means investing only some of your money in just one stock or type of investment. Diversifying your investments is critical. Imagine if you only played one video game your whole life—boring, right? The same goes for investing. Mix it up to keep things exciting and safer.

You won't believe it! Investment apps are all the rage now, like the Snapchat of the financial world. They're ultra-cool and user-friendly, offering excellent features and easy-to-navigate screens. You can jump-start your investing adventure with just a tiny amount, maybe even the change you find in your pockets! But remember, these apps have pros and cons like anything else, so making an intelligent choice when selecting the one that suits you best is essential.

Parents, pay attention! You have a crucial part to play in this journey. By guiding your teenagers and creating custodial accounts (yes, those exist!), you can assist them in making intelligent investment decisions. It's like being the trusted co-pilot on their financial adventure.

Lastly, why not make learning about investing a fun family activity? There are financial camps for teens where you can learn about investing through hands-on activities and workshops. It's like summer camp but with an economic twist!

How to Establish Attainable Goals

Setting realistic goals is a crucial skill, especially for teenagers facing the ups and downs of adolescence. Here's a helpful guide to help you become skilled at establishing and achieving your objectives.

Begin With Dreams, Then Set Goals

Remember, goals are not just over-glorified wishes. They are dreams with work boots on! Before setting a goal, identify what you dream about. Is it acing your next math test, saving for a cool gadget, or starting a YouTube channel? Dreams are your destination; goals are the journey to get there.

Embrace the Power of WOOP and SMART Goals

Let's talk about two powerful goal-setting strategies: WOOP and SMART. WOOP stands for wish, outcome, obstacle, plan. It helps you envision your goal (wish), imagine the best outcome (outcome), identify potential hurdles (obstacle), and devise a plan to overcome these challenges (plan).

Next is SMART: specific, measurable, achievable, relevant, and time-bound. This method ensures your goals are clear, easy to track, doable, meaningful, and have a deadline.

Start Small and Build Confidence

Begin with manageable goals to avoid feeling overwhelmed. For instance, if you're eyeing an A in science, start by setting a goal to study for 30 minutes daily. Small wins lead to significant victories!

Make Your Goals Passion-Driven

Passion is like the fuel that keeps your engine running. Whether you're super into saving the planet or crazy about basketball, make sure your goals match what gets you pumped. You'll find it easier to stick with your goals when genuinely passionate about them, even when things get challenging.

Money Matters: Financial Goal-Setting

Becoming financially responsible is a big deal, starting with setting impressive goals. How about saving some of your allowance, budgeting for that fabulous prom dress, or forming your small business adventure? These goals aren't just about saving money; they're like your practice field for mastering money management and showing off your self-discipline skills. It's time to put your money to work and achieve fantastic financial feats!

Use Resources and Tools

Utilize apps and websites dedicated to goal-setting. They offer structured guidance and help track your progress—and they're free!

Don't Go Solo

Tell your friends, family, or mentors about your goals. They can provide support and guidance and even team up with you. Remember, when you share a goal, the effort becomes more bearable, and the joy doubles!

Embrace Flexibility

Life is unpredictable. If you hit a roadblock, reassess and tweak your goals. Adaptability is a superpower in the world of goal-setting.

Celebrate Every Step

Acknowledge every milestone, no matter how small. Celebrating progress keeps you motivated and gives you a sense of achievement.

Remember, Failure is a Stepping Stone

Don't sweat it if you mess up; every slip-up is an opportunity to grow, bringing you nearer to reaching your dreams. Embrace your blunders as valuable lessons to cherish.

Keep the End in Mind

Remember your initial motivation. It will be your anchor, keeping you on course and laser-focused, even when faced with distractions or obstacles.

Setting achievable goals involves dreaming big while taking small steps, staying passionate yet adaptable, and rejoicing at every milestone. So, put those goals ahead and bring your dreams to life. The world is eager to see what you can accomplish!

The Significance of Periodically Reviewing and Modifying Objectives

First, setting clear investment goals is like having a treasure map—it gives you a path to follow and ensures you don't get lost in the wild world of stocks. It's not just about making money; it's about creating smart money moves that match what you want in life, whether a new car, college fund, or a giant pizza party! Research shows that having specific and challenging goals can boost your performance much more than just a "do your best" attitude.

Imagine the stock market as a thrilling rollercoaster with highs, lows, and unexpected twists. That's why watching your financial goals and closely adapting them when necessary is essential. Consider this: You initially began investing to get a new gaming console in a few years, but now you're aiming for something bigger, like saving up for college. Your investment decisions should grow and change along with your aspirations!

And remember, it's not just your goals that can shift—the market itself can be unpredictable. Tech stocks could be skyrocketing one moment, and the next, they might slump. Having a diverse portfolio is like assembling a team of superheroes, each with unique abilities. Just like you wouldn't want a team entirely made up of Hulks, avoiding putting all your money into one type of stock is essential. Instead, mix it up with different companies and industries to keep things in balance and reduce the chance of your investments taking a nosedive.

Let's talk about the superhero squad of your portfolio—different stocks and bonds. You've got your value companies, the underdogs that might surprise you with a comeback; small companies, the rookies with considerable potential; and companies with high profitability, the steady and reliable ones. Regular check-ups on your portfolio help determine if you need more underdogs, rookies, or steady players to hit your goals.

Remember to monitor the expenses associated with investing, like fees and commissions. Just as you would want to avoid blowing all your allowance on a single game, you should aim to minimize investment costs. By reducing these costs, you ensure that more money stays in your pocket, ready to grow for your future goals.

To wrap it up, think of managing your investment goals like being the captain of a ship. You've got to set the right course, adjust the sails when the winds change, and keep an eye on your crew (your stocks and bonds). By doing this, you're not just sailing aimlessly but on a thrilling adventure to Treasure Island, aka your financial goals. Remember, in the stock market game, the players who keep learning and adapting are the ones who win the treasure!

Key Takeaways

- Understanding and managing investment risks is essential, like a financial shield against market unpredictability.
- Building long-term wealth means using clever investment tactics and harnessing the enchanting power of compound interest.

- Setting financial goals and milestones helps map your investment journey, adapting as your dreams and the market evolve.

- Having a variety of investments is like mixing up your financial strategy, just as you balance different foods in a healthy diet to keep your money game strong.

- Regularly reviewing and adjusting investment strategies is crucial, just like a captain steering a ship through changing seas.

- Compound interest in investing acts like a snowball effect, growing your wealth over time.

- Financial goal-setting for teens involves starting small, using tools, and embracing flexibility.

- Revisiting and tweaking investment objectives ensures alignment with personal ambitions and market changes.

You've just unlocked the basics of dodging investment risks, planting seeds for long-term wealth, and charting your course with financial goals and milestones. Pretty cool. But there's more! Let's level up and dive into the world of critical financial concepts. Think of it as adding secret weapons to your money-managing arsenal. We're talking budgeting, understanding stocks and bonds, and the art of savvy spending. You need these power-ups to navigate the financial universe like a pro.

Chapter 5:

Key Financial Concepts

Money matters might sound like a maze, but fear not—I'm here to make it as clear as your favorite TikTok dance. In this journey through the world of finance, we'll uncover critical concepts that will help you become a money-savvy superstar.

From understanding taxes and their impact on investments to navigating the ethical side of the stock market, I've got you covered. We'll even dive into budgeting, saving, and the exciting world of investments. Buckle up as we explore how financial literacy empowers you to make wise choices and align your beliefs with your financial portfolio. Let's make dollars and sense!

Key Financial Concepts

Let's dive into some cool money ideas like making a budget, saving, and investing. It's not just about having cash for that fantastic concert or the latest game; it's about setting yourself up for a rockin' future!

To begin with, let's tackle budgeting, which is all about managing your money like a pro. Imagine it as charting your financial journey. Start by identifying your income, which includes earnings from jobs, allowances, and perhaps some birthday gifts. Next, list your expenses, such as phone bills, snacks, and fun date nights. Grab a fantastic budgeting worksheet and start monitoring. The key is to understand what you have and where it's flowing. It's akin to steering the helm of your financial adventure!

Saving money isn't just for grannies and grandpas. Consider this: If you start early, you'll have more of the big stuff later. College? Traveling? A fancy gadget? Yep, you can save for all of that. Did you know the average college student borrows about $30,000 for college (Gobler, 2023)? By saving early, you're dodging a big debt bullet right there.

Now, for the exciting part: investing. It's not only for dudes in suits. Investing can be your ticket to making your money grow. It's like cultivating a money tree and observing it unfold. You can start small, and those investments can add up over time. You're making your money work for you, and who wouldn't want that?

How Financial Literacy Helps People Make Wise Financial Decisions

Let's delve into a topic of utmost significance that is often underestimated: financial literacy. It's not merely about stashing away a few dollars; it's a transformative force that can shape your future!

First, did you know that financial literacy has a massive impact on wealth? A study found that the most financially literate folks had a median net worth of over $225,000, four times more than those at the bottom of the financial literacy scale (Eli, 2021). Mind-blowing, right?

You might think, *But why does this matter to me as a teenager?* Here's the deal: Learning the ropes of personal finance now sets you up for a killer future. Sadly, only about 24% of millennials understand basic financial principles, and 87% of teens admit not understanding their finances (Radic, 2023). That's where you can change the game!

Imagine this: You're chilling, watching YouTube, and stumble upon a video like *How to Make Money as a Teenager*. Suddenly, you're hooked on personal finance—just like that! YouTube, books, and blogs are your treasure trove of financial wisdom. Books like *Think and Grow Rich* by Napoleon Hill or *Your Money or Your Life* by Joseph R. Dominguez offer deep insights into the world of money (Eli, 2021).

Now, let's talk action. Start with a simple budget. Track your expenses for a bit, and then plan your spending and savings. Remember, saving is vital! As a teen, you've got the golden opportunity to save a good chunk of your income.

And here's something cool: Investing isn't only for adults. You can start building your wealth empire early with a custodial account.

The bottom line? Financial literacy isn't about counting pennies; it's about making smart choices that lead to a secure and prosperous life. So, dive into learning about money management, and who knows? You might just be the next financial guru among your friends!

Everyday Life Examples to Illustrate Financial Principles

Let's dive into personal finance with some incredible insights and real-world examples. It's not merely placing money in a piggy bank; it's about becoming skilled in handling finances.

- **Budgeting and Saving:** Imagine earning $200 monthly from your part-time gig. It's wise to save a chunk of it, like 20% ($40). Why? Because emergencies happen, or maybe you're dreaming of a killer spring break trip. Take Emma, a high school student who puts away 30% of her babysitting cash for college. Smart move, right?

- **Credit and Debt Management:** Credit cards have the potential to act as a two-sided blade. Use them wisely, and they're your BFF. Mess up, and it's trouble. Learn from Jake, who always clears his credit card balance each month. This way, he avoids those nasty interest charges and keeps his credit score shining.

- **Living Below Your Means:** Here's a fun challenge: Try not to spend every penny you make. Let's skip that pricey concert for a chill night in. Or, like many, live with a roommate to slash those rent costs. The goal? More money in your pocket and less stress.

- **Setting Savings Goals:** Picture this: You want a $1,000 vacation next year. Break it down, and you must save about $83 per month. It's like a financial puzzle, and you're putting the pieces together one month at a time.

- **Don't Wait to Invest:** Having an early start is wise because of compound interest. It's akin to planting a money tree and witnessing it flourish with even more money. Isn't that pretty awesome?

- **Build Skills and Multiple Income Streams:** Whether mastering a new language, coding, or starting a YouTube channel, learning new skills can open doors to earning more money. Diverse income streams mean you're not just relying on one paycheck. Imagine having a side hustle like pet sitting or vlogging—extra cash, anyone?

- **Understand Gross vs. Net Pay:** That first job paycheck might not be as big as you think. Why? Because of taxes and deductions. So, always plan your budget around what lands in your bank account rather than the dream amount.

- **Good Debt vs. Bad Debt:** Not all debt is evil. Student loans? They can be a ticket to a high-paying job. Always keep in mind the importance of balance. Avoid getting overwhelmed by excessive debt. While credit cards can be helpful, use them wisely for maximum benefits.

- **Start Building Credit Now:** A good credit score is like a golden ticket to better financial deals. Think lower interest rates and better chances of landing that dream apartment. But be careful—late payments and high balances can hurt your credit score.

- **Get Creative With Wealth Building:** The world is your financial oyster. From starting a business to "house hacking" (think buying a house and renting out rooms), there are many ways to grow wealth. Be smart, be creative, and watch your bank account thank you.

Remember, these are just the basics. Dive into resources to ramp up your money game. Starting sooner sets you on a path to greater financial well-being.

Understanding Taxes and Investment Implications

Think of your investments like a garden—you plant seeds (money) and hope they grow (make more money). But, just like a garden where some of your harvest goes to feed the squirrels (taxes), a portion of your returns might go to taxes in the investment world.

In 2023, there are seven federal income tax rates: 10%, 12%, 22%, 24%, 32%, 35%, and 37% (Durante, 2022). Your investments, whether stocks, bonds, or a lemonade stand, can be taxed differently based on how much you earn and what type of investment it is.

Let's say you've invested in stocks that've grown in value—awesome, right? You could encounter capital gains tax when you sell those investments at a profit. This is like having a super successful lemonade stand but needing to pay a bit to your local council to run a business.

Now, it gets more interesting with things like retirement accounts. For example, with a 401(k), you don't pay taxes when you put money in but do when you take it out after you retire. Think of it as sowing a seed and not worrying about the squirrels when it's time to reap the harvest.

Also, high inflation can be a bit of a party pooper. It can decrease the actual value of your tax deductions over time. This implies that your investment may not achieve the expected level of tax efficiency. It's like believing you have a whole pie to yourself, but inflation takes a slice before you even start eating.

Tools like TurboTax don't only calculate your potential investment taxes; they also prevent you from paying more than necessary. Additionally, they offer guidance in case your investments face an audit.

Every investor's situation differs, and tax rules can be as complex as a maze. However, grasping these fundamentals can equip you with the skills to navigate the realms of investments and taxation.

Tips on Tax-Efficient Investment Techniques

First, consider accounts like 401(k)s, IRAs, and HSAs as your financial BFFs. Why? They're like magical chests that let your cash grow without getting nibbled away by taxes. For instance, 401(k)s and traditional IRAs allow you to pay taxes later, not now, on what you stash away. Plus, if you're considering college, a 529 plan is like a piggy bank that grows tax-free for your education expenses.

If you've got a job and are wondering what to do with your 401(k) when you leave, go for a direct rollover to another tax-advantaged account. It's easier and avoids tax headaches.

Now, let's talk investments. Regarding taxes, it's important to note that not all investments are equal. Take, for instance, index funds and ETFs (exchange-traded funds); they resemble low-maintenance companions. They don't trade much, so they keep tax costs low. Mutual funds? They're the social butterflies, dealing a lot and potentially upping your tax bill.

And hey, don't forget about bonds! Municipal bonds can be tax-free, making them an intelligent choice for taxable accounts. Treasury bonds? They get a break on state and local taxes but not on federal.

Real estate and life insurance can also be your tax-saving allies. Investing in real estate offers deductions and favorable capital gains tax treatment. Life insurance, on the other hand, can grow your money tax-deferred, and you might even get tax-free payouts.

Lastly, donating to charity can score some tax deductions if you feel generous. Giving away stocks or property that have increased value can be especially tax-smart.

With these tips, you're on your way to becoming an investment guru. Remember, the world of finance is vast and constantly changing, so keep learning and stay curious!

Why It's Crucial to Keep Up With Tax Legislation

Let's discuss why keeping up with tax legislation is as crucial as acing your TikTok dance challenges. First, tax laws are constantly changing, like your favorite social media algorithms. For instance, in 2024, states have been refining laws on taxing online sales and considering retail delivery fees due to increasing online shopping trends and environmental impacts (Cole, 2023).

Imagine saving up for that dream gaming console or makeup palette, only to find out you've got extra taxes or fees to pay. Bummer, right? Knowing these changes helps you plan your spending and savings better. It's like being in the loop with the latest fashion trends but for your wallet!

Also, some states have a rise in retail delivery and bag fees. So, when ordering that late-night snack or new outfit online, these fees could sneak up on you.

And here's a quirky fact: Sales tax holidays are becoming a big deal. In 2023, there were at least 45 of them across 24 states (Cole, 2023). They sound great for snagging deals, but they can also be tricky. Some stores might hike prices during these holidays, so always be on your toes.

Being tax-conscious is akin to advancing your skills in a video game. You're better prepared, can save money, and won't be caught off guard by new laws. Plus, it's a great way to impress your friends with smart money moves.

Issues of Ethics in the Stock Market

Let's talk about the moral side of investing—because, let's face it, your money choices can impact the world in significant ways.

Investing goes beyond profits. It involves making decisions that reflect your values, like selecting a pair of sneakers. You consider the price tag and pay attention to their production process and environmental impact, correct? The same goes for investing.

- **The ESG Revolution: Environment, Social, Governance**

In 2023, something called ESG (environment, social, governance) will be the talk of the town in investment circles. Companies face scrutiny not only for their profits but also for their treatment of the planet, their people, and their business practices. But here's the twist: Some folks are not fans of this. For example, states like West Virginia and Texas have laws against investing in firms that don't support fossil fuels or firearms (Malone et al., 2023). It's like the investment world's version of a Marvel movie—full of conflicts and controversies!

- **"Greenwashing"—All Talk, No Action**

Imagine a company that talks a big game about saving the planet but, in reality, does very little. That's greenwashing for you. It's like saying you're a top-tier gamer because you once won a solitaire game. In 2023, some companies might do more "greenhushing" than greenwashing, keeping mum about their eco-efforts to avoid backlash (Malone et al., 2023).

- **Ethics in Profit-Making: Winners and Losers**

Here's a brain-tickler: When investing, does someone else permanently lose when someone wins? If you sell a stock for more than you bought, someone else might miss out on those extra bucks. It's like trading Pokémon cards—sometimes you score a rare Charizard, sometimes you don't.

- **Being the Change: Ethical Investment Choices**

Now, let's talk action. How can you, as a teen investor, make ethical choices? Start by doing some detective work on companies. Investigate their environmental objectives, how they treat their employees, and their contributions to society. Investing in a company is like voting with your wallet for what you believe in. You know what's cool? Ethical investing can be just as profitable as the conventional type. It's like choosing a veggie burger over a beef one—good for you and the planet!

- **The Big Players: Setting an Example**

Big investment firms, like BlackRock, are also stepping up. They're pressuring companies to reduce emissions and be more transparent. It's like your favorite influencer promoting recycling—it gets everyone talking and acting.

- **The Future Is In Your Hands**

Finally, remember, the future of investing is not just in the hands of big suits in boardrooms. You also hold the power, and even the smallest of your choices can create a substantial influence. It's like choosing to walk or bike instead of asking for a ride—every little bit helps in the grand scheme.

Investing isn't just about the greenbacks; it's also about the green earth. Make choices that make you proud and could help improve the world. And who knows? You may inspire the next generation of investors to think beyond profit.

Investors' Societal Responsibilities

Get ready for an exciting exploration because we're delving into the dynamic and essential realm of investors' societal roles. Hold tight because this isn't solely about generating wealth; it's about creating a positive impact!

Let's start with a mind-blowing fact: In 2024, over half of you, yes, 54% of global consumers, make shopping decisions based on a company's commitment to good deeds (CSR—corporate social responsibility) (Eser, 2023). That's huge! It means your choices in the mall or online can influence how companies behave. Imagine picking a pair of sneakers because they look fantastic and the company helps clean oceans—pretty awesome, right?

Now, think about this: 88% of consumers, just like you, actually take the time to check out a company's CSR initiatives before buying their products (Overvest, 2023). This is not just about boycotting the bad guys; it's about supporting the good ones—those companies that care about the environment, treat people fairly, and give back to communities. By doing this, you're not only buying a product but also voting for the world you want to live in.

Speaking of making a difference, did you know that a whopping 90% of S&P 500 companies now report on their CSR activities? Back in 2011, it was only 20% (Eser, 2023). This is a massive shift! Companies are starting to realize that being good is good for business. They're taking action because it's morally right and because individuals like you are observing them and making decisions based on their behavior.

But here's where it becomes even more astonishing. As future investors, you have the power to shape the business world. A study found that investors like you and me are willing to sacrifice some financial returns to invest in companies that are doing good things for the world (Hirst et al., 2022). You're investing in what truly matters to you!

Now, for the companies out there, listen up! CSR isn't just a fancy badge to wear. It's serious business. Brands that stand for something more than just profits outperform the stock market by a whopping 120%. And CSR can boost a company's market value by 4%–6%. Not to mention, over 40% of a company's reputation is tied to how socially responsible they are (Overvest, 2023). So, if you want to be a star in the business world, you better start thinking about more than just the bottom line.

Finally, let's not forget the environment. Sustainability and finance are now BFFs. We're seeing a massive shift where caring for the planet is becoming a core part of business strategy. This means companies are finding innovative ways to be kinder to our planet while making a profit.

Remember, your choices and actions have the power to change the world. It's not solely about earning money; it's about creating an impact. And guess what? You can do both!

How to Match Personal Beliefs With Financial Portfolios

Want to ensure that your money reflects your beliefs? You're in luck because matching your values with your financial portfolio is achievable and quite remarkable. Let's dive in and explore how you can put your money to work for both you and the world!

First things first, let's chat about what it means to invest according to your beliefs. If you have a solid environmental passion, consider investing in companies that wholeheartedly support green energy and sustainable practices. Or, you're all about social justice, so you'd look for companies prioritizing fair labor practices and diversity. The key is to find investments that reflect what's important to you.

Now, let's discuss how you can achieve this. One approach involves engaging in socially responsible investing (SRI). This means you're specifically looking for companies that meet specific ethical standards. It's like picking friends who share your values—but in the business world. Another approach involves impact investing, focusing on companies actively striving to impact the world positively. This is like joining forces with superheroes out there making a difference.

"But hold on," you might ask, "Do I need to give up earning money to make a positive impact?" No! Let's dive into why this is so intriguing. Companies focusing on social and environmental issues often perform well. Why? Because they're forward-thinking and they're tapping into what people care about today. Plus, by investing in these companies, you're helping to shape a better world.

Let's look at some examples. Say you're passionate about clean energy. You could invest in companies that are developing solar panels or wind turbines. Or, if you care a lot about health and wellness, you might invest in firms working on groundbreaking medical treatments or healthy living products.

You might think, *This sounds great, but I'm just a teen—can I get into this?* Absolutely! More and more financial services cater to young investors, helping you get started with investment accounts matching your age and interests. Plus, there are many resources online to assist you learn about different companies and how they align with your values.

One more thing: As you start this journey, remember that the world of investing is constantly changing. What's popular today may not remain the same in the future, and companies can adjust their practices, either for improvement or decline. So, keep an eye on your investments and be ready to adapt. Like staying in the loop with the hottest TikTok trends, you must remain alert and informed!

Matching your personal beliefs with your financial portfolio is a fantastic way to make your money matter. Investing in companies that align with your values can earn a profit and contribute to causes you care about. Begin your exploration, continue your learning journey, and remember, you could potentially emerge as a significant figure in ethical investing. Remember, your money, values, and impact—let's make it count!

Key Takeaways

- Budgeting resembles steering your financial ship as its captain, enabling you to monitor income and expenditures effectively.

- Early saving can help avoid college debt and prepare for future expenses.

- Investing has the potential to increase your wealth gradually, beginning with a modest amount and witnessing it accumulate over time.

- Financial literacy empowers you to make wise choices, with studies showing financially literate individuals have higher net worth.

- Learning about personal finance sets teenagers up for a prosperous future, and resources like books and online content can help.

- Understanding tax implications on investments, such as capital gains, helps navigate the world of finance.

- Tax-efficient investment techniques involve using tax-advantaged accounts and choosing tax-friendly investments.

- Keeping up with tax legislation is crucial to avoid unexpected tax burdens and plan spending and savings effectively.

- Ethical investing means making investment choices that reflect your values, considering ESG factors and companies' ethical practices.

- Investors have societal responsibilities as their choices can influence companies to prioritize CSR, leading to better corporate behavior.

- Matching personal beliefs with financial portfolios is possible through socially responsible and impact investing, aligning investments with ethical values.

- Companies focusing on social and environmental issues often perform well in the market, creating profit and positive impact opportunities.

You've just embarked on an exciting journey into finance, where you've learned about key financial concepts, taxes, ethical considerations in the stock market, and the power of making budgets, saving, and investing. Now, let's dive into some practical exercises for teen investors that will make your financial adventure even more thrilling!

Chapter 6:

Practical Exercises for Teen Investors

Prepare to turbocharge your investment journey with practical exercises, real-life teen investor stories, and savvy strategies to adapt to ever-changing markets. We're talking real deals, simulation games, and wisdom from the wins (and oops!) of others. It's time to master the art of intelligent investing!

Practical Exercises for Teen Investors

Let's dive into the exciting world of stock investing with practical exercises that'll reinforce the core principles and make you feel like a Wall Street whiz, even if you're still in high school. Investing isn't just for the suit-and-tie crowd; it's a skill you can start learning now in a fun and engaging way. So, buckle up. Here are some hands-on exercises to get your investing journey started!

- **Fantasy Stock League:** Imagine it like fantasy football, but in the world of stocks. Assemble a squad of friends and build a pretend portfolio. Using a spreadsheet, you can employ online simulators or keep tabs on your stocks. Choose a blend of familiar and unfamiliar companies. Monitor their performance for several weeks or months. You'll swiftly grasp how market trends, company updates, and economic developments influence stock prices. Diversification is vital—don't concentrate all your investments in a single basket!

- **Follow the News, Predict the Impact:** Start following financial news on a site like CNBC or Bloomberg. When big news hits—like a new iPhone release, a change in leadership at a major company, or an extensive economic report—jot down how you think this will affect the stock prices of relevant companies. Then, watch the market and see if you are right. This exercise will teach you how external factors influence the market, and you'll get better at predicting trends.

- **Budgeting for Investing:** Let's face it, you can't invest what you don't have. So, start a budget. Whether it's your allowance, part-time job earnings, or birthday money, figure out how much you can set aside for investing. It's not only about picking stocks; it's also about managing your finances responsibly. This exercise will help you not only with investing but also with your adult life.

- **Company Deep Dive**: Select a company that piques your curiosity and delve into it like a pro. Dive into their annual report, keep an eye on their stock performance over a few months, and explore who their rivals are. What drives this company's success? Is it turning a profit? How does it compare to its competition? This process will teach you the art of assessing a company's well-being and potential for growth, a vital skill for investors.

- **Investing Podcasts and Videos:** There are tons of great resources out there. Find a few investing podcasts or YouTube channels aimed at young investors. Listen or watch regularly. Not only will you learn the lingo, but you'll also start understanding the strategies and ideas that drive successful investing.

- **Interview an Investor:** Know someone who invests? It could be a family member, teacher, or a friend's parent. Ask them about their investing journey. What worked, what didn't, and why?

You'll gain insights from real-life experience, and it's a great way to learn from others' successes and mistakes.

- **Reflect on Your Emotions:** Investing can be an emotional rollercoaster. Start a journal and describe your feelings about your mock portfolio's performance. Are you panicking during a market dip? Are you overexcited about a sudden gain? Reflecting on your emotions helps you understand the psychological aspect of investing, which is just as important as the financial one.

Remember, the best investment you can make at your age is in your education and understanding of the market. These exercises are about making hypothetical money and building the skills and mindset you need to be a savvy investor. So, have fun, learn lots, and who knows? One day, you might be the next big name in the investing world!

Exercises Using Simulation to Make Investing Choices

Let's talk about the magic of stock market simulators—your secret weapon in mastering the art of buying low and selling high!

Picture a video game where you can trade stock without fearing losing money. This is precisely what a trading simulator provides—a digital training ground to grasp the intricacies of stock trading. Think of it as the training wheels that accompany your investment journey. These simulators replicate a lifelike market setting with all the functionalities of a real trading platform, and here's the kicker: No real money is at stake. So, you can experiment, make errors, and acquire knowledge without worrying about depleting your bank account.

Here's how it works: You'll have an order window to place simulated trades, just like in real-life trading. There's a charting application, indicators, and even a market scanner to give you the whole experience. You can test different strategies and see what works best for you in various market conditions—whether the market is going up, down, or sideways. It's like playing a financial version of Minecraft, where you build your trading skills block by block.

Now, how long should you play this game? Experts suggest at least 1,000 hours in the simulator (McDowell, 2022). Think of it like training for a marathon—the more you practice, the better you get. Remember, even Tiger Woods had to spend countless hours at the driving range to become a golf legend. Trading is no different!

You've got some excellent simulator choices! Take TradingSim, for example. It lets you go back in time and experience the stock market up to three years in the past—it's like having a stock market DVR! Or, check out TradingView's Bar Replay mode, where you can select the day and time and dive into virtual trading with user-friendly tools. It's simple, intuitive, and gives a natural feel for the trading universe.

eToro offers another excellent simulator, especially for beginners. You get $100,000 in virtual funds and can easily switch between your real and virtual accounts. It's perfect for testing the waters before diving into real investing.

TradeStation stands out as a top choice for active traders and won't cost you a dime. It provides real-time data, unlimited virtual trading funds, and comprehensive backtesting capabilities. If you prefer day trading, consider exploring NinjaTrader and TradeStation for their advanced functionalities and lifelike trading atmospheres.

Remember that employing these simulators isn't solely for enjoyment (though it's pretty enjoyable!). Instead, it's about enhancing your ability to recognize patterns and understanding which strategies excel in market situations. Think of it as progressing through levels in a game—each session boosts your competence as a skilled trader.

How to Draw Lessons From Successful and Unprofitable Financial Situations

Whether your portfolio is just a twinkle in your eye or you're already dipping your toes in Wall Street's vast ocean, here's the scoop on extracting priceless lessons from both your triumphs and not-so-triumphant moments in the stock market.

- **Embrace Your Inner Student:** Remember, being cool doesn't mean skipping school. Picture the stock market as a thrilling rollercoaster where you're in charge of the twists and turns. Begin with the fundamentals: Grasp the concept of stocks, understand how the market functions, and uncover the factors influencing price movements. Keep in mind that knowledge is your superpower, especially when it comes to managing your money wisely!

- **Start Small and Dream Big:** You can kick-start your investment journey without needing a fortune. Beginning with a small sum is a wise choice. Consider it like a trial run—just as you wouldn't purchase a car without a test drive, you can dip your toes into stocks with a modest amount to grasp the basics of investing.

- **Diversify, Diversify, Diversify:** You may have heard the wise saying, "Avoid concentrating all your assets in a single place." This valuable guidance applies to the stock market as well. Diversify your investments by allocating them across various stocks, industries, and even types of assets. Doing so ensures that if one investment performs poorly, your overall portfolio remains resilient and unaffected.

- **The Crystal Ball Doesn't Exist:** Spoiler alert: No one, and I mean no one, can predict the stock market with 100% accuracy. So, if you dream of finding that magical formula to pick winning stocks every time, it's time to wake up and smell the coffee. Investing is about making educated guesses rather than crystal-clear predictions.

- **Learn From Your Losses:** Let's talk about those not-so-great moments. You buy a stock and it sinks like a rock instead of shooting to the moon. Ouch! But here's the deal: There's a treasure trove of lessons in those losses. What went wrong? Did you follow the herd without doing your homework? Did you ignore red flags? Reflect, learn, and tweak your strategy.

- **Celebrate and Analyze Your Wins:** On the flip side, when you score a win, throw a mini-party (you deserve it!), but then get down to business. Why did this stock do well? Was it luck, or did your research pay off? Understanding what you did right is as essential as understanding what went wrong.

- **Keep an Eye on the Taxman:** Taxes might not be the most exciting subject, but they're incredibly significant. Remember that Uncle Sam is entitled to a share of your profits. Therefore, remember to include taxes when calculating your earnings, as they can significantly impact your overall returns.

- **Patience Is a Virtue:** Finally, it's worth remembering that creating a successful stock portfolio takes time, just like Rome didn't happen overnight. Investing is a long-term journey, not a quick sprint. Don't let temporary market ups and downs dishearten you. Stay focused on your goals and stick to your plan.

Armed with these tips and a dash of patience, you're well on your way to navigating the stock market like a pro. Remember, every investor started somewhere; now is the best time to start.

Case Studies of Teen Investors

We have some fantastic real-life stories of teen investors who've made waves in the stock market. We'll dive into their strategies, explore their savvy moves, and extract some golden lessons from their journeys.

Successful Investors Who Started Stock Investing in High School

Dylan Jin-Ngo

Let's dive into the case study of Dylan Jin-Ngo, a teen stock market enthusiast. At just 17, Dylan discovered his passion for investing in sixth grade. His journey began with self-learning and soon led him to become the nation's youngest certified mutual fund counselor in 2020 (Ferré, 2021).

Dylan established Young Investors Corp, a non-profit organization collaborating with Boys and Girls Clubs in Los Angeles and Orange County to boost financial literacy. While he shows interest in well-known stocks such as Tesla and Apple, he cautiously approaches market highs. His initiatives have benefited more than 350 students, and Dylan actively supports implementing statewide financial literacy programs. Dylan's achievements demonstrate that one's age doesn't hinder financial expertise, and he is reshaping youth financial education standards (Ferré, 2021).

Advait Arya

Let's dive into the world of Advait Arya, a young, ambitious trader making waves with his intelligent investment strategies. At just 16, Advait started his journey during the COVID-19 lockdown. With a seed capital of Dh8,000, he embraced online resources like Investopedia and insightful YouTube videos to sharpen his market acumen (Nair, 2021). His primary trading platform? eToro, where he keenly observed trends and replicated successful trades.

Advait's approach is cautious yet savvy. He prefers stable, long-term investments in giants like Amazon, Apple, Google, and Facebook, steering out volatile stocks. Why? Because high school keeps him busy, and thorough research on unstable companies demands time he can't spare. Despite this, he's not afraid to take calculated risks, investing in

Electronic Arts and betting on their next-gen technology to revolutionize gaming.

Here's a fascinating twist: Advait isn't only about making profits. He channels his earnings into Defy, his non-profit, supporting the underprivileged across five countries. His secret to success? Start with a demo account, learn from mistakes, and research thoroughly before investing. Remember, in Advait's world, knowledge is as valuable as gold.

Brandon Fleisher

Let's dive into the case study of Brandon Fleisher, a savvy young investor who started his journey in the world of stocks back in eighth grade. Thanks to a math class project, Brandon got hooked on investing. He picked a stock, Avalon Rare Metals, and watched it soar. Fast forward, Brandon, just 17, was managing an actual portfolio with $48,000 of his parents' money, growing it to $147,000 (Bowsher, 2015). His strategy? Focus on small-cap stocks and do thorough research.

Brandon didn't just stick to textbook methods. He actively sought out CEOs of small companies, learning directly from the source. He even created a website, thefinancialbulls.com, to share and discuss investment ideas with other young enthusiasts. His approach was simple: Understand your investment and stay committed to your research. This strategy paid off well. He turned his parents' $50,000 into $110,000 in less than two years (Cazzin, 2015).

You might find Brandon's story inspiring. He shows that with curiosity, a willingness to learn, and a lot of research, even the stock market can become a playground for success. Remember, as Brandon says, don't invest in what you don't understand. Always think outside the box.

Lessons Learned From the Experiences of Peer Investors

Grab your notepads and let's unpack some golden nuggets from the stories of Dylan, Advait, and Brandon. Here's what you can learn:

- **Start Early, Like, Really Early:** Dylan caught the investment bug in sixth grade. If investing sounds more remarkable than the latest TikTok trend, you're on the right track.

- **School Projects Can Lead to Big Things:** Brandon turned a math class project into a passion for investing. Next time you groan about a school assignment, remember it could be your ticket to Wall Street!

- **Embrace Self-Learning:** Dylan didn't wait for a college degree to enter the stock market. You can become a stock market whiz from your bedroom with resources galore online.

- **Think Big, Start Small:** Advait initiated his journey with a mere Dh8,000, proving that you don't require a substantial sum to commence. Even a modest allowance can serve as the ignition for your investment expedition.

- **Balance Risk With Homework:** All three wonder kids did their homework before investing. Sure, chasing high-risk stocks might seem thrilling, but slow and steady often wins the race.

- **Not Just for Profits:** Advait's Defy initiative demonstrates that investing involves more than accumulating wealth. It also allows you to contribute positively to the community using your earnings.

- **Networking Is Key:** Chatting up CEOs like Brandon did might sound daunting, but it's all about learning from those who've been there and done that.

- **Dabble in Different Markets:** Whether it's tech giants or small-cap stocks, exploring various sectors can be fun and educational.

Remember, age is just a number in investing. Curiosity mixed with daring can take you places!

Modifying Investment Approaches With Time

Like in the most incredible video games, the financial market keeps changing, and you must adapt your strategy accordingly. Here's a walkthrough for tweaking your investment plans when the market acts up or your financial goals do a one-eighty.

Initially, keep in mind that your investment strategy remains flexible and adaptable. It resembles a dynamic document that adjusts as you mature and external circumstances shift. Consider it your financial navigation system, consistently reevaluating the optimal path to your desired economic objectives.

- **Step 1: Check Your Financial GPS**

Did you get a new job or a pay raise, or decided to save for a cool new gadget? Time to reassess your financial plan! Our financial goals change and so should our investment strategies. Maybe you're now aiming for a bigger goal (like a car or college fund) or adjusting your timelines. This isn't just about growing up; it's about growing smart with your money.

- **Step 2: Risk Tolerance—Are You a Financial Daredevil or Safe Player?**

Your risk tolerance is like your gaming style—some love high-risk, high-reward boss battles, while others prefer accumulating points steadily. You should play it safer if you're nearing a big financial goal (like college). But if you're in for the long haul, you might lean toward stocks that have the potential for higher returns, even if they fluctuate more.

- **Step 3: Performance Check—Level Up or Game Over?**

Monitor the performance of your investments closely. If they're not performing as expected, investigating why is essential. Remember that a bad day in the market shouldn't prompt you to exit hastily. Investing is a long-term journey, but if your investments consistently underperform or perform exceptionally well, it's prudent to analyze the reasons and make strategic adjustments accordingly.

- **Step 4: New Levels, New Challenges**

Sometimes, the investment world changes—new rules, players, and games. This could mean new opportunities or risks for your investments. Stay informed and be ready to adapt. Your investments should evolve with the market, and your life changes.

- **Step 5: Get a Co-Player (Financial Advisor)**

Even top gamers occasionally seek assistance or guidance. If you require support with your financial decisions, think about consulting a certified financial planner (CFP). They resemble a knowledgeable mentor in your financial journey, providing specialized advice tailored to your monetary circumstances and objectives. They can assist you in navigating intricate financial terrains and providing perspectives you may have yet to explore.

- **Step 6: Remember, It's Your Game!**

Most importantly, you're the player here. Your investments should match your personal financial goals and values. Whether investing in stocks for quick gains or building a diversified portfolio for long-term growth, ensure it aligns with your financial objectives and journey.

Importance of Routine Review and Adjustment of Stock Portfolio

Investing in stocks can be quite a ride, especially when starting. Your funds are at stake, and you aim for them to grow. However, it's crucial to remember that the market shifts and your financial objectives evolve. This is why regularly examining and adapting your portfolio is as vital as selecting the perfect Instagram filter for your awesome selfie.

First off, what's a portfolio? Picture it as your financial backpack. Inside, you've got a mix of investments—stocks, bonds, and maybe some mutual funds or ETFs. Just like you wouldn't pack the same stuff for a beach day as for a snowboarding trip, your portfolio needs different things at different times.

Picture the market as a colossal game of musical chairs. Every so often, the tempo of the music (reflecting market conditions) swings from a lively beat (during a bull market) to a sad tune (in a bear market). As the music shifts, it's crucial to rearrange your investments to avoid being caught without a chair when the music fades.

Why review your portfolio? Simple: Things change. Companies that were the "next big thing" can become yesterday's news. Industries evolve, new technologies emerge, and economic conditions fluctuate. Regularly checking in on your investments ensures you're still on track to meet your goals, like buying that dream car or funding your start-up.

Your life transforms. What you want at 15 might be worlds apart from what you want at 25. You may be saving for college now, but consider starting a business or traveling the world in a few years. Your investments need to match your changing goals.

So, what's the ideal frequency for reviewing your portfolio? Picture it as your routine dental check-ups. Conducting it twice a year is a solid guideline. But remember, don't just glance at it and consider the job done. Delve into it! Are your stocks delivering the expected results? Is your comfort level with risk still intact? Are there fresh opportunities that warrant your attention?

Adjusting your portfolio may involve either a substantial restructuring or minor fine-tuning. It might entail selling underperforming stocks and increasing investments in those showing promise. Alternatively, you might opt for greater diversification to mitigate risk.

Keep in mind that investing is individualized. What might be effective for your friend may not necessarily suit your unique financial aspirations and risk tolerance. Like a fingerprint, your portfolio should reflect your dreams and goals, akin to your distinct financial identity.

Think of routinely reviewing and adjusting your portfolio as the GPS for your financial journey. It helps you stay on course, avoid potholes, and find a shortcut to your financial goals. Keep an eye on it, make intelligent adjustments, and who knows? You might be the next big success story in the world of investing!

Case Studies Showing Successful Adjustments of Tactics Under Changing Market Conditions

Listen up! I've got some excellent insights from real-world investors who've made their portfolios shine even when the market was having its rollercoaster ride. Let's break it down with case studies showing how savvy investors adjust their portfolios under changing market conditions.

Spicing Things Up With McCormick & Company

So, there's this company called McCormick—yes, the one that probably spices up your kitchen. Investors watching McCormick's stock noticed something remarkable. Its price/earnings (P/E) ratio and other financial metrics fluctuated predictably during growth cycles. When McCormick's stock price dipped below its usual pattern—for example, in 2014, when sales growth slowed—savvy investors saw an opportunity to buy (*McCormick & Company - A Case Study*, 2016). They grabbed the stock at these lower prices, and, spoiler alert, they made a neat profit when the stock bounced back.

Think of it like waiting for your favorite video game to go on sale—you grab it at a lower price and enjoy the same incredible experience.

Navigating Choppy Waters With Russell Investments

Here's another strategy from the big brains at Russell Investments. They used fantastic tactics in their funds—"quality income" and "U.S. defensive value." Quality income is like adding a steady player to a sports team. They focused on companies with solid financials and consistent dividends, which is like picking players who score consistently. The U.S. defensive value was their way of balancing the team, adding players who were undervalued but could still bring solid game.

These strategies helped them manage risks and grab opportunities, especially during the wild ride of the COVID-19 pandemic. For instance, as growth stocks got super expensive, they shifted toward cheaper value stocks. This move paid off big time, especially during the market turmoil in 2022 (*Completion Portfolios Case Study*, 2023).

Imagine you're building a fantasy sports team. You want a mix of consistent scorers and underrated players who could surprise everyone. That's what these investors did with their portfolios.

The Art of Rebalancing With Bloom Advisors

Lastly, let's discuss the importance of maintaining a balanced portfolio. Picture this: You begin with a mix of stocks and bonds, say 60% stocks and 40% bonds. If stocks perform well, you might end up with more stocks than intended, say 75%. This alters your risk profile. To return to your initial plan, you should rebalance—sell some high-performing stocks and purchase more bonds. Think of it as fine-tuning your sailboat to navigate smoothly in your chosen direction, even when the wind shifts. This approach helps you buy when prices are low and sell when they're high, effectively managing risk while striving for solid returns.

It's like playing a video game where you constantly adjust your strategy based on your challenges. You don't stick with the same moves; you adapt to keep winning.

Key Takeaways

- Engage in hands-on exercises to build your stock market skills.

- Utilize stock market simulators to practice trading strategies without financial risk, gaining experience in a realistic market environment.

- Draw inspiration and lessons from teen investors who started young and achieved success.

- Modify your investment tactics as market conditions shift to match your evolving financial objectives.

- Continuously assess and modify your investment portfolio to match your changing financial goals and market dynamics.

- Study real-world case studies to understand how experienced investors adjust tactics under various market conditions.

After the practical exercises for teen investing, let's switch gears and zoom into the digital age of investing. Imagine your smartphone and laptop as your new financial sidekicks. We're diving into how technology can be your secret weapon in investment research. In the next chapter, learn to tap, swipe, and click your way to savvy investing!

Chapter 7:

Using Technology for Investment Research

Diving into investment research is a breeze with cutting-edge tools at your fingertips. Have you ever heard of robo-advisors? These are your digital finance buddies, automating investments and making life easier for teens like you. But hold on, it's not all about making easy money.

Cybersecurity is a big deal—you must keep your financial and personal data locked down tight. I'll show you how to navigate the endless sea of online resources, tap into data analytics for intelligent investment decisions, and integrate tech-driven solutions into your strategy. And, of course, we'll talk about staying safe online because your security is as vital as your profits.

Using Technology for Investment Research

Are you eager to jump into the thrilling realm of investing? Good news! You can access many internet resources and tools to guide your decision-making process. Let's explore some excellent resources to guide your investing journey!

- **Stock Market Apps:** Apps like Robinhood, Webull, and E*TRADE are perfect for beginners. They offer easy-to-understand interfaces, educational content, and even the ability to start with small amounts of money. For example, you can buy a fraction of a share in a company like Apple, even if you don't have hundreds of dollars to spare.

- **Investment Blogs and YouTube Channels:** There are tons of experts and enthusiasts sharing their knowledge online. Channels like *The Financial Diet* and blogs like *Investopedia* provide articles, videos, and tutorials on investing concepts. They break down complex terms into simple language.

- **Stock Screener:** Use stock screeners on Finviz or Yahoo Finance to sift through stocks efficiently. These tools enable you to apply filters such as price, market cap, or industry, assisting you in honing in on potential investment choices that align with your criteria.

- **News Websites:** Keeping up with the latest news is crucial for investors. Websites like CNBC and Bloomberg provide real-time updates on financial markets, trends, and economic developments.

- **Social Media:** Surprisingly, platforms like X (formerly Twitter) and Reddit can be excellent sources of information. Loads of investors use these platforms to share their wisdom and experiences. Just remember to keep your guard up and verify the info you come across—the internet doesn't always play by the truth playbook.

- **Investment Forums:** Websites like Seeking Alpha and Stocktwits allow you to connect with other investors, discuss strategies, and get insights into individual stocks.

- **Online Courses:** You can find a wealth of investing courses on platforms like Coursera and Udemy, with many available for free. These courses offer a great way to establish a strong investing foundation.

Advice on How to Use Technology to Keep Up With Industry Developments

Harnessing technology is crucial in the fast-moving world of investing. It can be a significant game-changer, keeping you ahead in the industry. Let's explore the reasons and methods for leveraging tech to stay updated with the latest market trends and developments.

Why Use Technology?

- **Instant Information:** With the power of the internet, you can get real-time updates on your favorite stocks and markets. Apps like Robinhood, E*TRADE, or even Google Finance provide you with the latest news and stock prices at your fingertips.

- **Data Analysis:** With technology at your disposal, you can analyze stock trends like a seasoned pro. Utilize tools like StockCharts or Finviz to spot patterns, monitor performance, and set up alerts, helping you make well-informed investment decisions and stay one step ahead.

- **Research Tools:** Online platforms like Seeking Alpha, Yahoo Finance, and Bloomberg offer a wealth of information on companies, industries, and economic trends. You can read expert opinions, watch video interviews, and access research reports without sweat.

How to Use Technology

- **Mobile Apps:** Enter the game by downloading investing apps on your smartphone. They're super easy to use and come packed with excellent features. Take the Stockpile app, for instance. It lets you snag fractional shares of big-name companies starting at just $5. It's a fantastic way to invest without breaking the bank!

- **Online Courses:** Platforms like Investopedia and Coursera offer courses on stock investing. You can learn the basics and advanced strategies and even take classes on specific industries.

- **Social Media:** Follow financial experts on platforms like Twitter or YouTube. People like Warren Buffett or Elon Musk often share insights and news that can be valuable for your investment decisions.

- **Virtual Trading:** Use virtual trading platforms like Thinkorswim or TradingView to practice your skills risk-free. It's like playing a stock market video game but with actual data!

Data Analytics and Its Role in Enhancing Investment Decisions

Data analytics is an essential tool in the fast-paced world of stock investment. Banks and asset management firms are increasingly harnessing data-driven strategies to tackle economic challenges, including inflation and recession. These firms actively gather and scrutinize vast data sets, using them to shape well-informed investment decisions.

For you, as a teenager interested in stock investments, understanding data analytics can give you a significant advantage. Imagine you're playing a video game but with real-world stakes. Data analytics is like having a map that shows where the treasures (profitable stocks) are and where the pitfalls (risky investments) lie. By analyzing trends, market behaviors, and financial reports, you can predict which stocks might go up and which ones might not do so well.

In today's finance world, data is king. Major firms deploy advanced algorithms to sift through massive data sets, guiding their investment choices. As a beginner, your journey starts with mastering market trend analysis and the fundamentals of financial reporting. Mastering the investment game revolves around understanding its rules.

Remember, predicting the stock market's behavior often proves challenging. Data analytics can guide you, but they need to be foolproof. Stay flexible and eager to learn. Investing in stocks isn't just a path to profit; it's a journey toward financial savvy and a deeper grasp of the economic forces that mold our world.

Automation and Robo-Advisors for Teens

Let's talk about robo-advisors and how they're shaking up the investment world—think of them as your fantastic, tech-savvy money managers.

Imagine robo-advisors as your pocket-sized financial whizzes. These software tools tailor your investment strategy based on your preferences, like financial targets and risk comfort. Just fill in your details, and voilà, they conjure up a bespoke investment mix that's in tune with your style. Think of it as creating a custom financial playlist about you!

The cool part is that these robo-advisors monitor your investments 24-7. They automatically adjust your portfolio to align with your goals and risk level, especially when the market does its unpredictable dance. It's like having a financial bodyguard who's always on duty, ensuring your money works as hard as you do.

But here's the kicker: Robo-advisors are cheaper than traditional human advisors. They charge a small percentage of your investment, making them appealing, especially if you need to roll in dough.

There is an ongoing discussion about whether robo-advisors can entirely substitute human advisors. Some individuals express reluctance in entrusting their finances to machines. They contend that humans can grasp the intricacies of your life and provide guidance that machines cannot. Additionally, certain robo-advisory companies face profitability challenges due to their low fees and the modest size of client portfolios.

On the flip side, these digital advisors are perfect for those who want to dip their toes into investing without getting overwhelmed. They're super user-friendly, and you can check on your investments anytime, anywhere—from your phone or computer. Plus, as AI tech gets more intelligent, who knows what cool features robo-advisors will offer in the future?

Robo-advisors have revolutionized investing, making it more accessible and less intimidating. While they might only partially replace human advisors, they provide an excellent option for those who embrace technology and seek a cost-effective way to grow their wealth.

The future of robo-advisors looks bright, and they're worth checking out if you want to make your money work smarter, not harder!

Advantages and Restrictions of Automated Investing Services

Automated investing services, also known as robo-advisors, have become increasingly popular among teenagers and young investors. These digital platforms offer a range of advantages and restrictions that you should be aware of when considering whether to use them for your investment needs.

Advantages

- **Low Fees:** Robo-advisors usually have lower fees than traditional financial advisors, allowing you to keep more of your money invested, which can lead to long-term growth.

- **Diversification:** Automated investing services spread your money across various assets, reducing the risk of putting all your eggs in one basket. This diversification helps you weather market ups and downs.

- **Accessibility:** You can access robo-advisors through your smartphone or computer, making it easy for teenagers to start investing with just a tiny amount of money—no need for hefty initial investments.

- **Customization:** Robo-advisors employ algorithms to craft tailored investment portfolios, considering your financial objectives, comfort with risk, and investment horizon.

- **Hands-Off Approach:** They require minimal effort on your part. You don't have to monitor the stock market or frequently make decisions constantly—your robo-advisor handles this for you.

Restrictions

- **Limited Human Interaction:** Robo-advisors don't offer the personal guidance of a human financial advisor and can't provide emotional support or address specific financial queries.

- **Cookie-Cutter Portfolios:** While customization is a strength, some robo-advisors may offer limited investment options, leading to a one-size-fits-all approach.

- **Lack of Control:** Automated investing may not be your cup of tea if you're a DIY enthusiast. You need more control over specific investments.

- **Market Risk:** Robo-advisors are not immune to market volatility. During severe market downturns, your investments can still suffer losses.

- **Tech Reliability:** Your investment management depends on technology, and any technical glitch or cybersecurity problem could jeopardize your funds.

Although robo-advisors are popular in managing investor assets, you should carefully study the pros and cons. Moreover, consider your financial goals before diving into automated investing.

Tips on How to Include Tech-Driven Solutions Into Your Stock Investing Approach

Some exciting choices await you if you want to explore stock investing through tech-driven apps. Let's delve into a few of them.

Let's begin with Acorns, an excellent choice for beginners with limited funds. Acorns rounds up your everyday expenses to the nearest dollar and invests the leftover change on your behalf. Remember to monitor the fees, especially when your account balance is small.

Next, E*TRADE is excellent if you're serious about stocks, ETFs, or mutual funds. Although more affordable options exist, it earns high marks for its outstanding mobile app and customer support. Plus, it has an extensive selection of investments.

Mint is the essential app for sorting out your finances before investing. It aids in monitoring your expenditures, setting up a budget, and handling your bills. With a user base of more than 15 million individuals in the United States and Canada, it's the go-to tool for maintaining financial control (Ashworth & Enomoto, 2019).

Motif Investing employs data science and automation to craft thematic portfolios, which is ideal for individuals keen on thematic investing. You can kickstart your investments in these portfolios with as little as $300 (Ashworth & Enomoto, 2019).

Millennials love Robinhood because it offers commission-free trading in stocks, options, and cryptocurrencies, making it user-friendly with an active user base of more than 4 million (Ashworth & Enomoto, 2019).

SoFi, or Social Finance Inc., offers Stock Bits, which lets you buy fractional shares of popular stocks. This is perfect if you want to invest in expensive stocks with just a tiny amount of money.

Stash is another app you might like. It lets you start investing with as little as $5 and offers fractional shares in companies and ETFs (Ashworth & Enomoto, 2019). It has a subscription model with three different monthly plans.

Lastly, Wealthsimple is a robo-advisor offering ready-made investment portfolios. It's big in Canada and is expanding in the United States and the United Kingdom. They also launched Wealthsimple Trade for commission-free investing in stocks and ETFs in Canada.

Investing always carries risks, and educating yourself about these risks is vital. It's also essential to have clear financial goals and understand your investments.

Cybersecurity and Online Safety

As a teen investor looking to make your mark in the stock market, it's crucial to be aware of the cybersecurity challenges of using the internet for stock investing. The digital world offers incredible opportunities but presents risks you must navigate wisely. Let's delve into these cybersecurity issues, equip you with knowledge, and share real-world examples to help you stay safe and secure.

Understanding the Cyber Threat Landscape

The internet is a vast and interconnected space where cyber threats lurk at every corner. For teen investors, these threats can manifest in various forms:

Phishing Scams

Phishing scams aimed at teen stock investors pose a significant danger. Scammers frequently employ misleading strategies to deceive you into conveying personal and financial records. They might send counterfeit emails or messages that mimic trusted stock trading platforms or investment companies, often seeking your login details or sensitive information.

Take this scenario: A scammer might email you, pretending to be a famous investment app, alleging a security problem with your account.

They'll push you to hit that link for a quick fix, but that link? It's a trap, leading to a fake site itching to snatch your login info.

Malware Attacks

Hackers can employ different methods to target teenage stock investors with malware attacks. They might employ phishing emails or counterfeit websites to deceive teenagers into downloading harmful software. Once this software is on your device, it can steal vital financial information, like your login details for trading platforms or bank accounts. Additionally, it can track your online actions and jeopardize personal data.

Imagine a teenager downloading an investment app that promises fast and easy profits, unaware that it's a sham. Unbeknownst to them, the app contains malware that can access their financial accounts and compromise their investments.

Social Engineering

Social engineering can target teen stock investors by using deceptive online tactics to manipulate them into making financial decisions that may not be in their best interest. These tactics, such as "spear phishing," "watering hole attacks," and "baiting," are designed to trick individuals into revealing personal information or taking actions they wouldn't usually take online.

For example, imagine you're a teen stock investor who uses a popular trading app like Robinhood. Scammers might send you fake emails or messages that appear to be from Robinhood, asking you to verify your account by clicking on a link and entering your login credentials. If you fall for this phishing attempt, your account could be compromised.

Furthermore, social engineering can exploit the enthusiasm of young investors when it comes to stock investing. It's vital to be cautious and verify the legitimacy of any communication related to your investments.

Weak Passwords

Using weak passwords is a significant danger for teenage investors in the stock market. It can make you an attractive target for hackers aiming to breach your investment accounts and gain access to your financial details. Consider the example of passwords such as "123456" or "password123"—these are typical weak passwords that hackers can easily crack.

Hackers target teens because they may have less experience with online security. They could gain unauthorized access to your stock trading accounts, manipulate your investments, or even steal your money.

Real-World Examples

- **Robinhood Data Breach**

In 2021, Robinhood, a widely used stock trading app, faced a data breach that exposed the personal details of millions of users. This event underscores the significance of online platforms implementing strong security measures and emphasizes users' need to actively watch over their accounts for any signs of suspicious activity.

- **Pump-and-Dump Schemes**

Cybercriminals use social media to artificially boost the prices of specific stocks, often targeting teenagers who tend to follow online trends. Engaging in thorough research and avoiding making impulsive investment choices influenced by social media hype is crucial.

In the digital world, where exciting opportunities await teen investors, safeguarding your investments and personal information becomes paramount. You can confidently explore this online terrain by staying well-informed and adopting sound cybersecurity practices.

Remember that the financial landscape and cybersecurity risks are constantly changing. Ensure your safety, stay informed, and embrace your adventure as a teenage investor in this digital era.

Safeguard Your Financial and Personal Information Effectively

In the current digital era, stock investment has become highly accessible to teenagers, thanks to the proliferation of online trading platforms. Initiating your investment journey requires just a few clicks. Nonetheless, staying mindful of potential risks is crucial, particularly when securing your financial and personal data. This guide offers valuable recommendations for protecting your information while you work toward your investment objectives.

Choose a Secure Platform

When choosing an online trading platform, make security your top priority. Seek platforms with solid encryption and two-factor authentication (2FA) to safeguard your login credentials. For instance, platforms like Robinhood and E*TRADE use 2FA for extra security.

- **Example:** Robin is a teenager who wants to start investing. He chooses a platform like Charles Schwab because it provides robust security features like 2FA and encryption.

Beware of Phishing Scams

Phishing scams involve fraudulent efforts to acquire your sensitive information, typically using fake emails or imitation websites that resemble legitimate ones. Always exercise caution by avoiding clicks on dubious links and refrain from sharing personal information online.

- **Example:** Emily received an email claiming to be from her brokerage firm, asking for her login information. She didn't click the link and instead contacted her brokerage directly to confirm the email's legitimacy.

Use Strong Passwords

Craft distinct and robust passwords for your trading accounts, steering clear of predictable ones such as "123456" or "password." A potent password should blend letters, digits, and special characters.

- **Example:** Jake relies on a password manager to create and save intricate passwords for his trading accounts.

Regularly Monitor Your Accounts

Remain watchful by regularly monitoring your investment accounts for any signs of unauthorized transactions or unusual activities. The quicker you detect an issue, the sooner you can address it.

- **Example**: Sarah reviews her account statements monthly and immediately reports any discrepancies to her brokerage.

Be Wary of Public Wi-Fi

When accessing your investment accounts, steer clear of public Wi-Fi networks since they might lack security if you have to make transactions while moving. Use a virtual private network (VPN) to enhance your online security.

- **Example:** Alex uses a VPN connecting to his investment accounts from a coffee shop's Wi-Fi.

Educate Yourself about Investment Scams

Take the time to learn about common investment scams and red flags. Be cautious of anyone promising guaranteed high returns with low risk, as these often become scams.

- **Example:** Chris avoids investing in a "get rich quick" scheme that promises extraordinary profits without risk, recognizing it as a classic scam.

Secure Your Devices

Ensure you actively install the latest antivirus software on your devices for stock investing and consistently update security patches. Regularly update your operating system and applications to address any security weaknesses.

- **Example:** Lisa updates her smartphone and computer with the latest security patches.

Limit Sharing on Social Media

Exercise caution when sharing your investment activities on social media, as excessive sharing can make you vulnerable to scammers. Refrain from revealing specific information about your holdings and financial situation to maintain your online security.

- **Example:** Max refrains from posting about his investment portfolio on social media to protect his privacy.

Stay Informed

Keep yourself updated on cybersecurity threats and best practices to stay informed and effectively defend against potential data breaches.

- **Example:** Daniel regularly reads articles and watches videos on cybersecurity to stay current.

Investing in stocks can be thrilling and potentially lucrative for teenagers, but it's essential to prioritize the security of your financial and personal information. By heeding these tips, you can reduce the hazards of online investing and concentrate on building your wealth confidently.

Remember that safeguarding your data is necessary for a thriving and safe investment journey.

Suggestions for Safe Internet Conduct to Safeguard Young Investors

As a teenager exploring the intricate realm of the internet, particularly in the context of investing, it's vital to remain well-informed and exercise caution. The internet provides numerous opportunities for education and investment but also comes with dangers. Here are some essential recommendations for young investors like you to ensure safe online behavior.

- **Understand the Digital Investment Landscape:** The internet has created fresh investment opportunities, mainly due to the emergence of cryptocurrencies and the influence of social media figures on financial choices. Acknowledging that these platforms provide valuable insights and carry inherent risks is crucial. Exercise caution when seeking investment guidance online, and discern trustworthy sources. Remember that not all online information is dependable or driven by good intentions.

- **Stay Informed About Online Risks:** It's alarming to know that children as young as seven use social media, and teenagers spend an average of eight hours a day on screens, excluding online classes. This increased exposure can lead to various risks, including online exploitation and exposure to inappropriate content. Make sure to educate yourself about these risks and how to avoid them.

- **Use Social Media Wisely:** Platforms like TikTok, Instagram, and Google have implemented various safety measures and educational resources to protect young users. TikTok, for instance, has a version for users under 13 that restricts posting. Instagram introduces tools for parents and guardians to monitor and guide minors' usage. Google encourages positive internet behaviors through initiatives like "Be Internet Awesome." Leverage these tools and resources to stay safe.

- **Follow Parental Guidance and Maintain Open Communication:** Parents and guardians have a vital role in guaranteeing safe internet usage. Collaborate with them to understand devices and applications and utilize parental control features as needed. Maintaining open communication regarding internet safety is essential. If you ever come across something on the internet that doesn't seem right or makes you uncomfortable, make sure to have a chat with your parents or a trusted adult about it.

- **Be Proactive in Online Safety:** The NSPCC and Childline assist children and teens facing distressing online situations. They offer confidential counseling and tools such as the Report Remove tool to eliminate inappropriate online content. Feel free to contact these resources if you require assistance.

- **Educate Yourself About Digital Etiquette:** Recognize the significance of being digitally civil. Demonstrate respect and politeness when you're on the internet. Remember that your actions in the digital world can have enduring consequences.

As a young investor in the digital age, it's crucial to be vigilant, informed, and proactive about your online safety. Remember, you must use the internet wisely and responsibly, as it's a robust tool for learning and investing.

Starting Small and Growing It to a Large Account

Before we end this chapter, let's talk about your exciting journey in stock investing. Growing a small savings into a large account for a life of financial freedom is an exciting journey, and it's possible with smart investment choices and patience. As a teenager, this might sound like a lot, but think of it like leveling up in a game. Begin with modest steps, maintain consistency, and focus on achieving financial independence.

First, let's talk about the power of investing in stocks. You've probably heard of companies like Apple, Nvidia, Chipotle, Microsoft, Google, and Amazon. These stocks have seen phenomenal growth over the years. If you had invested early in Apple, your investment would have seen remarkable growth. The tech giant started with a $22 per share when it went public in 1980 (*FAQ - Apple*, n.d.). On February 2, 2024, it closed at $185.85 (*Stock Price - Apple*, n.d.).

Here's an excellent way to think about it: Imagine buying just a few shares of Apple with your birthday money or savings from a part-time job. Fast forward to today. You could be sitting on a pretty impressive sum. The essence of successful investing lies in choosing the right stocks at the ideal time.

You might wonder, *How do I find the next Apple?* The trick is to look for themes in the market. Some of the current compelling investment themes include net zero, emerging market consumers, internet-driven business models, automation/robotics, artificial intelligence, and top brands. Companies operating in these areas and showing strong growth potential could be tomorrow's big winners. Think of investing in these themes as planting seeds that could grow into massive trees in the future.

But remember, investing is a long-term game. You're not looking to make a quick buck; you're building your wealth over time. It's like a strategy game where patience and smart moves pay off. Also, remember that despite common misconceptions, tech stocks can still perform well even when interest rates rise. Therefore, it's wise not to dismiss them hastily.

In summary, start by saving consistently, no matter how small the amount. Then, invest in stocks that align with solid market themes and show growth potential. And most importantly, be patient. Your journey to financial freedom is a marathon, not a sprint. Keep learning, stay informed, and watch your small savings grow into a large account that can support a life of financial freedom. Remember, the great stocks you invest in today could be the Googles and Apples of tomorrow!

Key Takeaways

- Investment research is accessible with tools like stock market apps, investment blogs, YouTube channels, and online news websites.

- Technology offers real-time information, data analysis, and research tools for keeping up with industry developments.

- In investing, data analytics means you analyze market trends and financial reports to make well-informed decisions.

- Robo-advisors automate investments based on user preferences, offering a hands-off approach to investing for teens.

- Automated investing services, or robo-advisors, provide low fees and diversification benefits but need more personalized advice and control.

- Tech-driven investing solutions for teens include apps like Acorns, E*TRADE, and Robinhood, offering features like fractional shares and budget management.

- Cybersecurity in online investing involves being cautious of phishing, malware, and social engineering and using strong passwords.

- Protect financial and personal data by choosing secure platforms, avoiding phishing scams, using strong passwords, and monitoring accounts.

- Safe internet conduct for young investors includes understanding the online investment landscape, being informed about online risks, using social media wisely, and engaging in open communication about internet safety.

- Investing in stocks like Apple, Nvidia, and Amazon can lead to exponential growth.

- Identifying future growth themes like Automation/Robotics and AI can lead to finding the next big winners.

- Tech stocks can still perform well in rising interest rate environments.

- Consistent saving and intelligent investment in growth-oriented stocks is crucial to building wealth over time.

Okay, savvy teen investors, we've navigated the tech-infused waters of modern investing, from using cool apps to dodging cyber sharks. Ready for the grand finale? Let's wrap this up with key takeaways to keep your investment journey intelligent, secure, and rocking!

Conclusion

As we wrap up this incredible journey through the world of stock market investing, let's take a moment to reflect on what we've learned and how it ties back to our objectives.

Objective 1: Providing a Solid Introduction

What an incredible journey it has been. Reflect on when the stock market felt like an entirely unfamiliar territory. Now, you've mastered the fundamentals and are handling them with expertise! From deciphering stocks and bonds to understanding dividends and market indices, that formerly daunting stock market terminology? You've got it all under control effortlessly.

With the confidence, knowledge, and excitement you've gained, you're ready to dive headfirst into investing. As you continue on this financial adventure, the possibilities are truly limitless. You're equipped with the tools and understanding to reach new heights. And let me tell you: The sky's not even the limit anymore; you've got what it takes to soar even higher.

Remember, every successful investor started somewhere, and you're well on your way. Keep learning, stay curious, and watch your investments grow. The future is full of promise, and you can seize it!

Objective 2: Equipping You With Tools and Skills

You have some seriously cool tools to rock the stock market in your virtual toolbox. Apps like Robinhood and Webull? Consider yourself a pro at navigating them to make savvy trades. You're not just swiping on your phone but strategically building your wealth.

Now, let's dive into the world of data analysis. It might sound sophisticated, but believe me, it's easier than you think! You'll become a pro at identifying trends and patterns, just like an experienced investor. Remember that it's not about intricate mathematics; it's about knowing the right time to buy and sell.

And those robo-advisors? They're like your trusty sidekicks, always ready to assist you in making informed choices without breaking a sweat. Consider them your financial superheroes, ensuring your investments stay on track even when the market does its rollercoaster dance.

With these powerful tools in your arsenal, you're well-equipped to take on the investing world with confidence and excitement. So, make those moves and watch your investment journey flourish. The future is bright, and your financial success is within reach!

Objective 3: Instilling Long-Term Wealth-Building

Now, let's delve into the core of investing—the long-term approach. You've refined your investment abilities and absorbed a critical concept: Amassing wealth isn't a short race but a continuous expedition. It necessitates patience, self-control, and a mindset focused on ensuring your financial future. Rather than pursuing rapid victories, you've aimed for economic independence.

And it's a genuinely motivating prospect! Envision a future where your investments consistently increase, providing you with the financial independence to pursue your aspirations and enjoy the benefits of your well-structured strategy. That's the remarkable goal ahead. It will be fantastic!

Maintain dedication to your chosen path, never stop acquiring knowledge, and witness your investments thrive. As you progress on this voyage, remember that each stride brings you nearer to financial stability and your imagined life. You possess the abilities, the mindset, and the resolve to turn your aspirations into reality. Keep up the outstanding effort!

But the stock market is a wild ride. You've learned that it can be a rollercoaster of highs and lows. Yet, armed with knowledge and the right tools, you're fearless in facing those ups and downs. You're a teenager with a plan, and that's pretty remarkable.

What lies ahead for you? Continue your learning, investing journey, and personal growth. Think of the stock market as a massive puzzle. You've already assembled some critical pieces. Remember that each decision you make now propels you closer to a financially stable future.

As you start this fantastic adventure, remember that you possess the expertise, the information, and the resolve to turn your financial aspirations into actuality. The investment realm is within reach, and your future appears more promising.

Whether embarking on your initial investment journey or advancing your expertise, this book is your reliable companion. Keep it within reach when you require additional assistance on your thrilling path to investment success. You're fully capable of achieving your goals!

References

Adam, J. (2023, July 24). *Experts predict how the stock market will perform for the rest of 2023*. Yahoo Finance. https://finance.yahoo.com/news/experts-predict-stock-market-perform-130011212.html

Ashworth, W., & Enomoto, J. (2019, July 17). *8 stock investment apps for young investors*. InvestorPlace. https://investorplace.com/2019/07/8-investment-apps-for-young-investors

Bowsher, K. (2015, April 28). *How a teenager tripled his money in the stock market*. Yahoo Finance. https://finance.yahoo.com/news/teenager-tripled-money-stock-market-190045942.html

Cazzin, J. (2015, March 20). *How I made $60,000 in investment returns*. MoneySense. https://www.moneysense.ca/magazine-archive/how-i-made-60000-in-investment-returns

Cole, G. (2023, December 11). *Tax law changes you need to know for 2024*. Avalara. https://www.avalara.com/blog/en/north-america/2023/12/tax-law-changes-you-need-to-know-for-2024.html

Completion portfolios case study. (2023, March 15). Russell Investments. https://russellinvestments.com/us/blog/completion-portfolios-case-study

Does market timing work? (2023, September 13). Charles Schwab. https://www.schwab.com/learn/story/does-market-timing-work

Durante, A. (2022, October 18). *2023 tax brackets and federal income tax rates*. Tax Foundation. https://taxfoundation.org/data/all/federal/2023-tax-brackets

Eli. (2021, June 25). *Why financial literacy matters for teenagers*. Teen Finance Today. https://teenfinancetoday.com/why-financial-literacy-matters-for-teenagers

Enomoto, J. (2024, January 1). *2023 Market recap: A year of surprises in stocks and sectors*. InvestorPlace. https://investorplace.com/2024/01/2023-market-recap-a-year-of-surprises-in-stocks-and-sectors

Eser, A. (2023, June 13). *Corporate social responsibility statistics in 2024*. ZipDo. https://zipdo.co/statistics/corporate-social-responsibility

FAQ - Apple. (n.d.). Apple Investor Relations. https://investor.apple.com/faq/default.aspx

Ferré, I. (2021, September 19). *Youth involved in the stock market 'is here to stay': Teen investor*. Yahoo Finance. https://finance.yahoo.com/news/youth-involved-in-the-stock-market-is-here-to-stay-teenage-investor-161706893.html

Fidelity study reveals teens think investing is important, but fewer than 1 in 4 have actually started. (2023, September 6). Fidelity Newsroom. https://newsroom.fidelity.com/pressreleases/fidelity--study-reveals-teens-think-investing-is-important--but-fewer-than-1-in-4-have-actually-star/s/fbe0e56c-bbf0-48d5-aa99-f9ce6282dae3

Fischer, M. S. (2021, November 8). *10 New findings on how investors pick an advisor*. ThinkAdvisor. https://www.thinkadvisor.com/2021/11/08/10-new-findings-on-how-investors-really-choose-advisors

Gobler, E. (2023, May 7). *Budgeting for teens: how to get started*. Clever Girl Finance. https://www.clevergirlfinance.com/budgeting-for-teens

Goodsell, D. (2020, June 14). *Four insights on the pandemic market and investor behavior*. Natixis Investment Managers. https://www.im.natixis.com/us/research/2020-financial-professionals-survey-pandemic-market-investor-behavior

Hirshleifer, D. (2020, July). *Behavioral biases of analysts and investors*. National Bureau of Economic Research. https://www.nber.org/reporter-2020-02/behavioral-biases-analysts-and-investors

Hirst, S., Kastiel, K., & Kricheli-Katz, T. (2022, October 24). *How much do investors care about social responsibility?* The Harvard Law School Forum on Corporate Governance. https://corpgov.law.harvard.edu/2022/10/24/how-much-do-investors-care-about-social-responsibility

Jacobino, N., & Akuffo, R. (2023, December 18). *How stock ownership and volatility will play out for 2024*. Yahoo Finance. https://finance.yahoo.com/video/stock-ownership-volatility-play-2024-171557150.html

Malone, L., Holland, E. B., & Simpson Thacher & Bartlett LLP. (2023, March 4). *ESG: Trends to watch in 2023*. The Harvard Law School Forum on Corporate Governance. https://corpgov.law.harvard.edu/2023/03/04/esg-trends-to-watch-in-2023/

Marder, A. (2023, December 12). *Americans mixed on 2024 economic outlook, plan to invest anyway*. NerdWallet. https://www.nerdwallet.com/article/investing/2024-economic-investing-outlook

McCormick & Company - A case study on portfolio management strategies (NYSE: MKC). (2016, December 4). Seeking Alpha. https://seekingalpha.com/article/4028100-mccormick-and-company-case-study-on-portfolio-management-strategies

McDowell, J. (2022, May 2). *Stock trading simulators for beginners*. TradingSim. https://www.tradingsim.com/blog/stock-trading-simulators-for-beginners-tradingsim

Nair, D. (2021, August 16). *How teenage traders are turning their pocket money into profits*. The National. https://www.thenationalnews.com/business/money/2021/08/17/how-teenage-traders-are-turning-their-pocket-money-into-profits

Outlook 2024 key takeaways. (2023, December 4). J.P. Morgan. https://www.jpmorgan.com/insights/outlook/market-outlook/2024-outlook-key-takeaway

Overvest, M. (2023, December 18). *Corporate social responsibility statistics 2024 — 65 key figures*. Procurement Tactics. https://procurementtactics.com/corporate-social-responsibility-statistics

Prince, D. (2022, November 7). *3 common mistakes investors make – and how to avoid them*. BlackRock. https://www.blackrock.com/americas-offshore/en/insights/common-mistakes-investors-make

Radic, D. (2023, February 28). *Astonishing financial literacy statistics for 2024*. Moneyzine. https://moneyzine.com/personal-finance-resources/financial-literacy-statistics

Riashi, J. (2021, May). *Why rebalancing your portfolio is so difficult*. Bloom Advisors. https://www.bloomadvisors.com/why-rebalancing-your-portfolio-is-so-difficult

Rose, S. (2023, September 6). *10 eye-opening financial literacy statistics*. OppLoans. https://www.opploans.com/oppu/financial-literacy/statistics-financial-literacy

Ryniec, T. (2022, January 26). *Lessons from 7 years of stock investing*. Nasdaq. https://www.nasdaq.com/articles/lessons-from-7-years-of-stock-investing

Sabatier, G. (2023, February 25). *Stock trading for teens: Best ways to start investing for teenagers*. Millennial Money. https://millennialmoney.com/stock-trading-for-teens

Stock Price - Apple. (n.d.). Apple Investor Relations. https://investor.apple.com/stock-price/default.aspx

Survey finds 93% of teens believe financial knowledge and skills are needed to achieve their life goals. (2022, April 4). Business Wire. https://www.businesswire.com/news/home/20220404005339/en/Survey-Finds-93-of-Teens-Believe-Financial-Knowledge-and-Skills-Are-Needed-to-Achieve-Their-Life-Goals

A teenager's guide to investing in the stock market. (n.d.). Luke Villermin. https://lukevillermin.com/books/teenagers-guide-investing-stock-market

2023 Teens and Money Study. (n.d.). TheNewsMarket. https://preview.thenewsmarket.com/Previews/FINP/DocumentAssets/648781.pdf

Waldron, D. J. (2023, May 6). *Why most investors underperform the market | Part 5: Timing the market.* Seeking Alpha. https://seekingalpha.com/article/4600851-why-most-investors-underperform-the-market-part-5-timing-the-market

Wise, H. (2023, October 19). *How to keep emotions out of your investment decisions.* Julius Baer. https://www.juliusbaer.com/en/insights/wealth-insights/how-to-invest/how-to-keep-emotions-out-of-your-investment-decisions

Made in the USA
Middletown, DE
30 August 2024